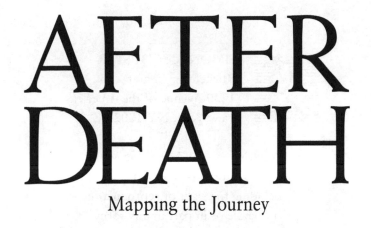

AFTER DEATH

Mapping the Journey

SUKIE MILLER, PH.D.

with Suzanne Lipsett

Simon & Schuster

SIMON & SCHUSTER
Rockefeller Center
1230 Avenue of the Americas
New York, NY 10020

SIMON & SCHUSTER and colophon are registered
trademarks of Simon & Schuster Inc.

Designed by Irving Perkins Associates

Manufactured in the United States of America

1   3   5   7   9   10   8   6   4   2

Library of Congress Cataloging-in-Publication Data
Miller, Sukie.
After death: mapping the journey / Sukie
Miller with Suzanne Lipsett.
p.   cm.
Includes bibliographical references (p. 213).
1. Future life.   2. Future life—Comparative studies.
I. Lipsett, Suzanne.   II. Title.
BL535.M48   1997
291.2'3—dc21   96-37338
CIP

ISBN 0-684-82236-9

In Memoriam

৵৵

This book is dedicated to the following family, friends, colleagues, and clients:

Joseph Unobskey (1883–1922)
Sara Rhea Unobskey (1880–1935)
William M. Unobskey (1903–1963)
Durval Barbosa (1931–1968)
Nicholas Gagarin (1945–1970)
Jason Lefer (1965–1980)
Joseph Unobskey (1932–1981)
Courtney Callender (1937–1984)
Dick Price (1930–1985)
Clement Bethel (1938–1988)
Arthur Lee Goldner (1956–1988)
Harry Sloan (1943–1988)
Susan Farrow (1945–1991)
Brendan O'Reagan (1945–1992)
Janet Lederman (1930–1992)
Lois Sivin (1952–1993)
Eunice Bethel Humblestone (1935–1994)
Camila Barbosa (September 17, 1994)
Suzanne Lipsett (1943–1996)

and to my mother,
Evelyn Unobskey Cutler (1913–1994)

Acknowledgments

This book would have been a very different endeavor without the inestimable and invaluable contributions of my Brazilian colleague Edmundo Barbosa.

I had long researched the afterdeath in interviews with experts and years and years of reading. My fascination with "what happens next" never diminished, but the work I was doing never came close to satisfying me or answering my deepest questions. I derived language, context, and points of view from my interviews and reading, but it wasn't until I met Edmundo Barbosa, a psychologist who worked with patients with terminal diseases, that the *experience* of the afterdeath actually jumped alive for me (a remark that will seem less strange, I think, by the end of the book).

Edmundo Barbosa's work and his locus, Brazil, where the dead are closer to the living than here, keep him hovering between life and death. Death and dying make up the bulk of his professional landscape, and he is accustomed to peering across into unknown territories. When we met I found that of all those I had spoken with in my interviews, of all those I had read, Edmundo Barbosa understood most intuitively what I was after: not only the intellectual speculation as to the nature of death and beyond, not only the religious projections and therapeutic comforts, but also the real, everyday concepts and images of the afterdeath woven into the living realities of cultures around the world.

Within a short time of our meeting, Edmundo began to accompany me on my visits to the peoples likely to have answers to my questions. Although he appears throughout this book as a fellow traveler into the afterdeath realm, I take this opportunity at the beginning of this journey to thank him with all my heart for his unique contributions to my project and to my thinking. Over the course of our work together, he and his wife, Iza, became personal friends and their son, Caio, became my godchild. But here my thanks are focused on the professional experiences in which this book is rooted: those long conversations about what we had seen, those slow interpretations of what we had heard, and those unforgettable moments of insight when one of us suddenly understood a most exotic message and could help enlighten the other. These mutual exchanges added a level of richness to the data, and thus to this book, that no amount of reading and talking could have done.

The Institute for the Study of the Afterdeath engaged many people around the world to gather its data. These senior researchers lived within the countries in question and had access to the particular group or groups we wished to learn from. Their roles and associations are described in more detail in Appendix B, but I want to thank them here and explain to the reader that, although they occasionally appear in the text of the book, they do not appear in a manner that reflects their constant presence and work, which made possible the steady exchange of information. The senior researchers were bridges—escorts, translators, explainers, interpreters—and this book could not have been written without their enthusiasm, talents, dedication, hard work, and many kindnesses.

It was in 1987 that I first had the idea to investigate the question "What happens to us after we die?" I knew without doubt that pursuing this question was the logical step in my own journey both as a psychotherapist and as a human being. But I wondered, would the results of such a pursuit be relevant beyond myself? Would they have potential meaning as well for the culture at large?

There was only one person I trusted to answer these questions, a proven bellwether of the culture and a man of astounding creativity, great breadth of knowledge, and discipline of mind. This was my longtime friend Michael Murphy, founder and chairman of the board of the Esalen Institute. I called and explained my idea. "Yes! Yes!" he responded immediately with his usual, life-infusing ebullience. "It's the next frontier! Do it!" Those words not only catalyzed the project but remained present in my mind when the ground was just too hard to sleep on, the careful travel arrangements came to naught, the funding ran out, and friends and colleagues looked askance. As always, Michael, thank you.

Thanks too to the late Brendan O'Reagan, of the Institute for the Noetic Sciences, who paved the way for me, introduced me to Edmundo Barbosa, and listened patiently to my hopes and fears. With great generosity he made available to me his encyclopedic knowledge of articles, books, and people. He argued. He probed. He approved and disapproved. I miss him very much.

This book could not have been done without the support of many people and a few critical institutions. I want to acknowledge the board and staff of the Fetzer Institute, who funded the early critical work of this project, as well as the Flow Fund, which, through its unique mandate, made me a better person. Thanks go as well to the Human Potential Foundation.

Ken Ring "got it" early on and made the difference. Charlotte Taylor's friendship, presence, and support added greatly to my peace of mind and the writing of this book. Irene Stampler bailed me out when I needed it most. Ute Stebich kindled in me the love of travel and the joy of the hunt, whether it be for art or information, and Gerhardt and Ute Stebich together helped immeasurably by scooping me up and taking me out of the city into the winter wonderlands. Stephanie Stebich cheered me on. The entire Stebich family was of great emotional and financial support.

Thanks to the following both for their ongoing interest and their financial support: Jack Himmelstein and Lauren Friedman, Bob Blau, Hilde Weisert, Helen Beck, Sally Whitcup, Lucy Waletsky, Lou Dunn Diekemper, Sandra Wright, Natalie Garfield, Ruth Fuller, Abraham Givnor; and my family, Martha and Dr. Fred Goldner, Sidney and Nancy Unobskey, and Ned and Sandy Ross. And my gratitude to "the old days" and the best eating club in the world; Jufies, Gary and Trish Friedman, Carole and Alan Becker, Lenore and Mel Lefer, and Bob and Marilyn Kriegel.

Several people were kind enough to read all or parts of the manuscript, and their feedback has, I believe, made this a far better book than it was. My deepest gratitude to John Levy, Bob Blau, Yvonne Rand, William Sterling, Stephen Mitchell, Marilyn and Bob Kriegel, Jack Himmelstein, Lauren Friedman, Cappy Cappaselo, Sheila Warnock, Eileen Rodgers Brady, Lenore Lefer, Carole Becker, Lee and Marty Moscof, Ute and Stephanie Stebich, Judy Skutch Whitson, Martha Goldner, and Abraham Givnor.

Thanks to Dick and Anne Grossman, who stood lovingly by from the very beginning, reading my early writings and repeating some of the most helpful and kindest advice I was to receive ("just keep going"), and to Stuart Miller, who coached, cajoled, scowled, and awarded gold stars as I struggled to find my voice and content. Lastly a bow of gratitude to the Ink Blots (you know who you are) and to Tony Minichoello for building me my dream house and office.

Joanna Slavin, secretary, bookkeeper, and all-around buddy, has generally held my life together for the past thirty years, and I want to take this opportunity to thank her for her loyalty and her many talents.

Gratitude to Tricia Nazabel, assistant par excellence, who made everything so much easier; Marcy Hyman, graphic artist and Director of BORIAL; Don Flint, sleuth and support par excellence; and Bob Roman, social psychologist and statistician, for taming the Research Grids. And to Joshua and Matthew Lefer, for taming my computer.

I am most grateful to my agent, Barbara Lowenstein, for her clarity, her enthusiasm, and her support; to Mary Ann Naples, who edited the manuscript with respect and insight, and a fine hand; and to Laurie Chittenden who truly assisted. Susan Heiken of Word Techniques patiently and accurately gave me final copy, more final copy, and final copy yet again. Suzanne Lipsett elegantly and gently midwifed it all into a book. Our work together was a joy. She was right; it was as if we had gone to summer camp together.

This book is about a journey to other countries, other peoples, other realms, and what I felt many times to be other worlds. Robin Van Loben Sels taught me about journeys. She was indeed the "inner companion on the journey," healing the old and making room for the new. Without her presence in my life I do not believe the idea to explore the afterdeath, much less its evolution, would have taken place. To her, I remain, as always, indebted.

SARA "SUKIE" UNOBSKEY MILLER

Contents

✥

AFTER DEATH

Introduction

⨳

"Men fear death as children fear to go in the dark," wrote philosopher Francis Bacon in 1625. Death and terror have always been companions—good reason for people to go about their everyday lives without contemplating the inevitable end. A few years after Bacon's pronouncement, in 1676 poet John Dryden offered a lyrical explanation for avoiding the issue: "Death itself is nothing," he wrote, "but we fear to be we know not what, we know not where."

For centuries, death has drawn the scrutiny of philosophers and poets. For the less reflective and literary among us there has always been a distinct turning away. Why study a mystery that yields so little? Why ask questions that have no answers? So it went for year after year: People of letters, of religion, of spiritual concerns contemplated death and its meaning in the greater reality, but those in the mainstream showed a great resistance to looking, wondering, and asking about death. Too close was the fearful darkness; too unnerving was the thought that not only our bodies but our very personalities, our *selves,* might disappear into nothingness at the moment of our death. Better to shut the darkness out by keeping the door slammed on death.

Something happened though, at the start of the 1970s, the beginning of the end of the age of denial. In 1969, psychiatrist Elisabeth Kubler-Ross asked the question: "What happens to us *as* we die?" In a series of detailed interviews with terminally ill patients, she set out to answer this question and then published her answers in *On Death and Dying,* the first book for lay as well as professional readers to reflect, open-eyed, on the dying process. Kubler-Ross's work was fruitful almost beyond precedent: She perceived a pattern to the dying process that has become one of the great organizing principles in our deepening understanding of death. Even more significant than a new way of seeing was Kubler-Ross's more fundamental contribution: She opened a door, turned on the light, and let the fresh air of day rush in on an all but unexamined aspect of reality. In doing so and writing of what she learned, she launched what has become a proliferating literature of death and dying.

A second pioneer in this dark, unexplored landscape took the next step by describing the threshold of the *after*death experience. Dr. Raymond Moody has documented the near-death experience, reported by 15 percent of Americans—people who have actually died but for a variety of reasons have returned to life. Whereas Kubler-Ross described the process leading up to death, Moody focused on what people experienced as they actually crossed the border. Like Kubler-Ross, Raymond Moody gave us a way of seeing, understanding, and talking about previously inchoate, indefinable experiences. By looking clearly, recording what they both saw and heard, and then seeking similarities among the reports that might lend insight to the whole, these two researchers created a language for perceiving what had previously been invisible. While Elisabeth Kubler-Ross asked, What happens to us *as* we die? Raymond Moody asked, What happens to us *when* we die?

Nineteen-ninety-four brought a fascinating variation on our hide-and-seek with death. "I have written this book to demythologize the process of dying," wrote Sherwin B. Nuland, in his book *How We Die*.[1] "Only through a frank discussion of the very details of dying can we best deal with those aspects that frighten us the most." The question Nuland took on was, "What happens to us *physically* when we die?" "It is by knowing the truth and being prepared for it that we rid ourselves of that fear of the terra incognita of death that leads to self-deception and disillusions."

After Death joins the growing literature that attempts to look closely at death and the afterdeath and their meaning for our lives. In doing so, it moves along this trajectory to ask the next question following Kubler-Ross's, Moody's, and Nuland's: What happens to us *after* we die?

I have been grappling with the question "What happens next?" my whole life. My father was a general surgeon who treated many cancer patients in the early 1950s, before the advent of radiation and chemotherapy. Every night at the dinner table, even when I was a very little girl, he and I discussed his cases. "Mrs. Cohn is recovering well from her surgery," he would report to me, and I, thrilled at the confidence, would try to nod sagely. Or he would tell me that "Mr. Cantor has crossed over." "But where?" I'd ask. "He's someplace else now," my father would answer. Another night, Mrs. Nelson, a patient we had discussed before, had also gone someplace else. I understood—or thought I did.

Someplace else was strangely familiar. Almost everything in my life was someplace else. The starving children in Europe were someplace else. The war was someplace else. My best friend, Madeline Keschen, who moved in the third grade, went someplace else. It was no stretch of the imagination to think that the dead went someplace else, too. When people went someplace else, there seemed to be no interruption in their existence as far as I could make out. My father's brothers, who visited frequently, certainly had a rich full life in the state of Maine; familiar guests returned from time to time; and the starving children in Europe did, in fact, grow up while the war progressed.

Raised quite near the border between life and the afterdeath, I was never encouraged to cover my eyes, look away, or hide from the questions of what happens to us after we die and where we go when we're no longer here. Among the many things my father gave me that stayed with me throughout my life were not answers to those questions, not pictures of a shadowy destination, but rather an enduring curiosity about and sense of safety surrounding that phenomenon he called "someplace else."

Decades after those dinner-table consultations with my father, as a psychotherapist with a busy practice and an abiding interest in the questions and issues that shape our psychological reality, I had occasion to consider that someplace else on a professional basis. Like many therapists nowadays, I found that a large number of my clients were people with chronic and terminal diseases seeking comfort, meaning, and ways to allay the anxiety related to their illnesses. That's when I found that even people at the brink of death frequently could not look at, ask about, reflect on, or wonder what was to happen to them after they died. These questions were all around me, and yet to a great extent they remained unexpressed.

So I began to wonder what other cultures, those more comfortable with the idea of death and freer about asking such questions, could teach us about the value of consciously contemplating the afterdeath. I knew that almost every culture throughout history encompassed in its belief system an idea of an afterdeath. Wide reading on the subject brought me into contact with detailed landscapes, even finely drawn maps of landscapes beyond life as we know it. I wondered what aspect of the human psyche was responsible and responsive to this information. Then I wondered if there were common threads, universal themes, that ran throughout all cultures.

As a way of beginning to investigate such questions and spurred by the deaths of a number of close friends and relatives and many clients in my practice, I began to envision a research institute that would collect rituals, myths, documents, oral traditions, art forms, and "afterdeath maps" of cultures around the world. Gradually the idea took shape. I learned the formidable skills of grant writing and fund raising, and eventually an organization—the Institute for the Study of the Afterdeath—became a reality, albeit a small one. Painstakingly, I assembled a group of prestigious researchers around the world committed to the concept of retrieving the diverse versions on the afterdeath in existence, and together, over the course of eight years, we collected detailed data in Asia, India, Indonesia, Brazil, the United States, and West Africa. Peoples who live in close contact with their dead give us conceptions of a world in which the border between life and death is highly permeable—where there is often no border at all.

The institute's goal has been to gather images and attitudes, beliefs and possibilities from around the world that might push back the limits on our view of the universe, bringing to our pragmatic Western viewpoint the often matter-of-fact view of the afterdeath that others have been experiencing for centuries. Far from urging Westerners to adopt the beliefs of the cultures studied, I intend merely to illustrate other perspectives on the human mysteries we all share. The point is not to proselytize but to permit appreciation of the many possible points of view alive today around the world.

Over the course of our field work, my colleagues and I have collected, if not a river, then perhaps an inland sea of material on what happens to us after we die. The many questions we have asked of our informants have been highly detailed, and the diversity of our interviewees' cultures has yielded an amazing range of responses.

How then do we compare, contrast, and, more important, plumb for meaning the multiplicity of descriptions of "someplace else" yielded by our senior researchers? How do we avoid the risk of reporting the data in an encyclopedic manner that lends itself to cataloging rather than inspiration and new understanding? Taking my lead from Elisabeth Kubler-Ross and Raymond Moody, I sought a pattern or patterns in the material we gathered—complete research questionnaires (multicolor coded), reproductions of art, extensive tape recordings, poems, photographs, Xeroxed articles, and more. Despite the wide range of differences in imagery and concept that seemed at first to be the data's most distinctive overall quality, a pattern indeed began to emerge.

As I contemplated the afterdeath systems, I found that many—even most—were not static locations, but rather active journeys, in which the spirits of the dead moved through detailed geographies. Even more exciting as I reflected on these journeys was the fact that despite their diverse cultural origins, they consisted to a greater or lesser degree of four separate aspects, or stages:

Stage I is the *waiting place,* where the traveler—the deceased— is transformed from a physical to a spiritual being in order to make the trip.

Stage II is the *judgment phase,* where the traveler's previous life is scrutinized and evaluated and his or her destination thereby determined.

Stage III is the *realm of possibilities,* where the traveler enjoys—or endures—the fruits of the judgment or, in systems where judgment is relatively insignificant, simply exists within the landscape of the after-death.

Stage IV is the *return,* or rebirth, where the traveler comes back to this life within the chrysalis of a new body and a new identity—or, alternatively, escapes the Wheel of Life to join the universal whole.

This four-stage system is not a rigid pattern to which every after-death system minutely conforms. For example, in some systems, there is no judgment whatsoever; in others, judgment is everything. In some, reincarnation is considered preposterous; in others it is inevitable.

I also began to see something hazier, something that had less to do with the afterdeath systems themselves than with how people gained access to them. People didn't simply think up and describe the after-death; some faculty—a particular way of apprehending—linked them to these landscapes and ideas. The work of the eminent philosopher and Islamic scholar Henry Corbin and others inspired by his writing helped me to focus on this capacity of the human psyche, difficult as it is to define and describe. This function, I began to understand, offered a way of considering the afterdeath, regardless of its particular content. I call this psychic function the vital imagination.

ABOUT THIS BOOK

After Death addresses that next question—"What happens to us *after* we die?"—by recounting the universal four-stage journey after death. Chapter 1 shows through living examples the importance of the question and provides the motivation for seeking answers from other cultures. Chapter 2 speaks to the power of the vital imagination, first in a highly personal way and then, in its concluding section, more theoretically. Each of the next four chapters is devoted to one stage of the afterdeath journey as discerned from the research data and described in cultures around the world. Chapter 7, the book's conclusion, focuses on hope as a psychological quality badly neglected by the scientific community and vitally necessary to people's moving through the stages and challenges of life and death.

The book ends with several appendices. Appendix A is a series of questions designed to allow the reader to define and assess his or her own afterdeath beliefs. Appendix B identifies and describes the groups whose afterdeath views we studied and introduces the institute's senior researchers who gathered data from them on our standardized 180-item questionnaire. Appendix C briefly describes the Institute for the Study of the Afterdeath, and Appendix D lists a selection of recommended reading in the field.

Here you have a bare-bones description of the book. However, visions of the afterdeath—their imagery, atmosphere, intimations of yet more—do not really fit neatly into carefully organized chapters. For this reason, I have embellished chapters with art, poems, and brief quotations set apart in boxes. Further, I have begun the four "stage" chapters with imagined fantasies of one simple version of the stage of the afterdeath to be addressed. In these ways, I am trying to provide not merely descriptions of the afterdeath but products of the vital imagination from many cultures. A book that is also a kind of imagery museum, *After Death* invites you to reflect on answers from around the world to the question "What happens to us after we die?"

PART I

OPENING TO THE
POSSIBILITY OF MORE

ೕ೫

The Next Question

Life is a great surprise. I do not see why death
should not be an even greater one.

—Vladimir Nabokov, *Pale Fire*

Where will I go when I die?
What will it be like when I get there?
Will I return to the living?
Will I disappear forever?

In the mid-1980s, two great friends and a client of mine died. They did not know each other and were as dissimilar as any three people could be. Yet in some way their experiences, and my experiences at their deathbeds, formed a complete whole. My friend Henry died in peace, facing the inevitable open-eyed and easing his friends along into the same intimate relationship with death that he was forging. My friend James died in anguish, afraid and bewildered, alienating most of those who cared for him, and clutching money to his breast as if it were the only means of saving him from the terrible unknown. My client Joanne had a need for just those ideas that were coming to occupy me increasingly at that time.

I was present at these deaths, was changed by them, and have long contemplated the lessons and insights, joys and sorrows, fears and mysteries that rose up in me at the bedsides. Many times over the ensuing years, in both my professional life as a psychotherapist who works with the terminally ill and in my personal life, I have felt grateful for these experiences. I am now involved in the work of describing the beliefs, images, and functions of the afterdeath in the cultures of the world. These three people brought me up close to this threshold.

FACING REALITY: THREE VIEWS

Henry

At age forty-five, Henry received the news that his newly discovered cancer was beyond treatment with a days-long silence, an integrating silence that allowed the reality to sink in. He was sad, he was un-characteristically quiet, and he withdrew from friends and family for more than two weeks while he consulted with physicians and healers of every stripe. All he saw confirmed the terminal diagnosis. Perhaps instinctively, he knew that to resist reality was to add to the inevitable pain and sadness of finding himself at the end of his life, but easing him into accepting reality was the fact that Henry believed there was more to life than met the eye.

During his period of withdrawal, Henry had his answering machine give out this message: "Do not call me unless you really want to. Do not call with any cures you know about. I have already tried them. Do not call with any procedures you know will work. I have investigated them. Do not call me if you are in any way confusing me with your dead father, brother, mother, friend, or whomever, and do not call me to cry and tell me how you will miss me. Call me if you can be there for me, and if you can't, it's okay. I send love."

I called Henry immediately on his inside line. "Oh, Hank," I said, using his nickname. "I'm so sorry."

"Didn't you get my message?" he asked with irritation. I had never heard Henry irritated but I knew it was to be expected.

"I got your message, but when another friend died, and I learned about . . ."

Henry cut me off.

"No, Sukie. Call when you can talk to me, not somebody else."

"Listen! It could help!" I pleaded.

"Sukie, I'm dying. I have six months. Stop," he responded.

I stopped. But if I couldn't help by being with him physically, if he didn't want "consoling," and if I couldn't offer information, there really was nothing I could say. I started to cry. Henry hung up. This was *his* trip, *his* death, *his* understanding of the human journey.

But I couldn't stop calling. The idea of losing touch with this man was simply intolerable—I wasn't going to let it happen. I called every day. Having poured my morning coffee and lit the best cigarette of the day, I would pull the phone to the couch, be sure the vase of flowers was placed in my direct line of vision so as to help calm me, and dial. Henry was always up early or never slept, I was never sure which, and each call found us individually perched and waiting: cautious, careful.

"So how are you?" I asked as soon as he answered. My tone was light, casual, as if this were an everyday call.

"Better," he responded, a smile in his voice. "I was just thinking that if I'd known in my twenties that I was going to die now, all that anguished stuff I went through in my twenties—remember?—would have been a mid-life crisis!"

I started to laugh. It was funny. Really funny and sharp. What he said was true in some crazy, witty, sweet way. He didn't at all avoid the fact that he was dying. The truth was there, but wrapped in something humorous that brought both relief from and acknowledgment of the truth. Not a man with a strict religious belief system inherited from his parents, Henry had evolved his own philosophy of the universe, its meaning, and the course of its evolution. His philosophy was one that would be familiar to many in the nineties: a combination of Christianity, Buddhism, and New Age spiritualism. Henry subscribed to an evolutionary model of the universe in which reality was continually moving toward a higher level of consciousness.

Henry had long believed in this forward progression and on a deep level felt himself to be part of it. When his doctor and the others told him sadly that there was nothing more to be done for him, what arose for Henry, through his shock and sadness as he told me later, was the understanding that he could evolve no further in his body and that it was time for him to move on to another level of consciousness. Henry contemplated what lay ahead and concluded that he had in some way been chosen, or assigned, to move on, and that there was meaning in his personal death. He was reflecting on ideas and hypotheses he had been thinking about for a long time, but now his thinking was far more intense than the intellectual browsing and musing that had brought him into contact with these ideas. In the face of death, his ideas were enlivened with a new urgency, a new longing. He asked, he looked, and he anticipated that he would cross boundaries of the unknown and search out alternatives to the unthinkable: the total and permanent disappearance of Henry.

Henry also believed in a hierarchy of beings, and that a host of manifestations of consciousness wiser and more highly evolved than ourselves awaited him after death. He had felt their presence, had meditated extensively in order to make contact with them, and so had confidence that he would be welcomed into a community—nothing clearly discernible, not even something easily imaginable, but still a collection of welcoming presences who would ameliorate the loneliness of leaving all his loved ones behind. It was a profoundly comforting idea to be moving toward a cluster of beneficent forms of consciousness as Henry gradually left the people he loved.

The members of Henry's family and all his friends were amazed at the equanimity with which he faced his death. Few of us shared his beliefs and many wondered how on earth these ideas could have arisen in the mind of a pragmatic New York businessman. But there was no mistaking Henry's curiosity as to what was to happen to him.

At the time of his death, Henry's family was there to witness its indisputable power in the visions it brought him and to give him comfort and ease. At the moment of his death, Henry opened his eyes and said with difficulty, "Oh, am I still here?" When told he was, he responded in a very weak voice, "Where I'm going is so beautiful."

James

James, who was forty-five when he died, had been raised in the Southern Baptist Church, with much music and constant reference to the life beyond death, to heaven and the presence of angels, to the Promised Land and a better life a'comin. But nothing of his religious upbringing had stayed with him or penetrated his spirit. James highly valued intellectual achievement and considered matters of the spirit to be childish fantasies. Long habit had left him with a rational explanation, dismissive disinterest, or a funny line for every aspect of reality that could not be fully explained. He grew up to be a very cultured man, spoke six languages, and was extremely well read, well traveled, well respected—he was the cultural commissioner of a large urban city and in touch with the many cultures that made up a great city.

Yet when death became inevitable for James, he found—to the surprise of all who cared for him—that he had no tools, no comforts, no healing thoughts. Far from wondering what he faced, what aspect of reality he was entering, James trembled and shied away. Regarding death, he had no access to meaning and certainly none to comfort or reassurance. The idea of his inevitable demise inspired nothing but sheer terror in his heart.

James's sufferings were unrelenting, and he placed enormous burdens on the people around him. With no sources of comfort within allowing him to accept, even for a moment, this inevitable phase of his life, James needed his friends and family to lavish on him unlimited soothing and attention. Though we longed to talk—just talk—James needed us to shoo away the terrors of the unknown, which rose up in the distinctly earthly forms they had always taken. His scariest bogeymen were fears regarding income taxes, ambiguities that may have crept into his will, insufficient insurance provisions. In his last days and hours, James obsessed about these legalities to the exclusion of all else—and to the exhaustion and frustration of those who hoped to sit with him and share a farewell.

For all his learning and his wide experience with the cultures of the world, James had no real referent regarding death other than the legalities that surrounded the end of a physical life. He was unable to wonder about or imagine a reality encompassing *more*—more than nothingness after death—and therefore, in his last days, found no doorway into comfort, meaning, or hope. In the face of death, all James knew was fear.

James was my best friend of twenty years, and I knew he had no hope of surviving his exotic cancer. It was not that I believed that this or that small dietary or body work idea would absolutely prolong his life. It was just that I wished—we all wished—that my most vital, responsive, fascinating friend could have remained, if he'd but tried, engaged by his life and not by his disease.

After a time, James just stared into space and wouldn't talk, but he needed "sitters." He could no longer be alone but he refused nursing care except at night. One sunny day I took a chance. It was July, but James was cold. The windows were closed and the odor of urine was heavy in the air.

"Where do you think you'll go if you die?" I finally asked, conceding to pretense by using "if."

"Cross town if I can get a cab," he snapped and closed his eyes to sleep.

My eyes were riveted on the extra pillow lying on a chair. Quickly, I sat on my hands. It had been a very long three years. I wanted to smother him with that pillow. I wanted the whole thing to be over. I wasn't proud of these feelings; instead, I was scared by them ("it's his death, not mine; it's his death, not mine," I chanted rapidly to myself), but his hopelessness was taking its toll. I had to make some space in the hot July air closing in on us: I could no longer breathe.

What hurt most about James's dying was not only the fact that he died but *how* he died. His loss to me was excruciatingly sad, and it was a tragic loss to all who had known that bright, brilliant, and gallant man. But in his dying he also damaged our love. I couldn't stand that absence of hope. I wasn't so foolish to ask hope of his doctors. I wouldn't have believed them anyway. I never had any hope that his belatedly diagnosed cancer wouldn't eventually defeat him. I knew better. But I wished *he* had hoped . . . for more.

For the record, from the moment Henry died of cancer, he was remembered with a vividness that never faltered. After a decade, there still isn't a third or fourth meal that friends don't say, "Oh, Henry would have loved this." He was a great fan of Chinese food, and many people laugh and see him at a Chinese restaurant in heaven. In fact, in his will Henry left $1,000 to his friends, directing us to take ourselves out to a huge Chinese meal, complete with Groucho Marx noses, a favorite accessory of his. We all remember Henry with great love and laughter, and we miss him in a very sweet way.

Nice stories. Different folks, different strokes. But I see much more than a variation in personal styles. I see an anecdotal argument for finally asking what happens to us after we die. Even in these stories drawn only from my personal life, I see persuasive arguments for overcoming cynicism and allowing the possibilities that death is a threshold rather than a door slammed shut and that the universe is a place of more than meets the eye. I see arguments for asking ourselves and encouraging our children to ask, "What's out there? Where do we go next? What happened to Grandpa and what will happen to me?" If we have no curiosity about what might exist after death, we blind ourselves to what many believe to be the next stage of our journey. "As far as we can discern," writes Jung in the chapter in his memoir where he explores his own dreams of life and beyond death, "the sole purpose of human existence is to kindle a light in the darkness of mere being."[1] We live with shadows, and too often in the dark shadows is death, but we have the opportunity to ask, to wonder, to consider— and to illuminate our own paths through reality's ever-present mysteries.

Think for a minute, or even longer as I did when first confronted with the following. What would it mean to you to believe as the Fon of the Benin Republic of Africa do that everyone and everything in the whole world belongs to groupings formed by the fact that their members die simultaneously? And that because these group members die at the same time, they all come back to life at the same time? Consider this idea, not as religious dogma, but in a moment of suspended disbelief as you might experience in reading a novel, watching a play, or reflecting on a poem.

Consider the implications of the idea of the Fon. According to them, if I were to die now, a whole fraternity of people and creatures—birds, foxes, lions, fish, men, women, babies, grandmothers, streams, clouds, insects, flowers, and trees—according to their own life schedules, would die with me. And because we died together, we would return together. Though we may be strangers, unknown to each other, we form a cohesive group, and that very group affords us the security of belonging.

For the Fon a single idea connects beings and things and people that are, if they're sentient, unaware of each other. It makes a community where before there were only unrelated individuals. True, we've heard a lot about the connectedness of all things in the universe, especially in the past decade or so, but like a beautifully rendered paragraph or verse, full of detail and color and rich description, this idea of the Fon brings specificity to that relatively abstract concept, and in that specificity each of us can imagine a place. This vision gives us the potential to delight in finding that all along we have belonged to some wonderful network of bugs, cats, and people, an unexpected fraternity that died when we died and returned to life when we did.

Something can happen if we visualize that interconnectedness and the detail it involves. Not only can our imagination fill with pictures, but almost without our noticing it—perhaps without our noticing it at all—the idea of death can become *normalized,* simply a part of a cycle shared by the wildly disparate members of our peer group. We could, perhaps, become accustomed to seeing death in a complex stew of reality, and if we did the world could become more precious, more comfortable, larger, more interesting—even far livelier and promising than the knowable world just this side of James's slammed door.

Joanne

Working with Joanne showed me the power that the mere exposure to ideas of the afterdeath carries. Joanne was a forty-five-year-old single mother and cancer patient whose disease had been managed successfully for eight years but who then began a sharp decline. She was petrified, and any allusion to her death elicited a storm of hysterical crying. She had not written her will; had not made provisions for her children; and had not discussed with her friends her hopes and desires for her children's welfare, her plans to have her work taken over, or her thoughts about her memorial service. Her crying and sobbing were like a wall between herself and her death—they kept her death from entering all conversation.

No one dared talk of death with Joanne, and the family finally decided to bring in a consultant: me. I asked Joanne directly, "What do you think will happen to you after you die?" Then I let her cry herself out, and finally she seemed to understand and accept that this was only a conversation.

"What? You mean after the funeral?" she asked. "What are they going to do with me after the funeral?"

"No, I mean something else. In many cultures people believe that very definite things happen after you die. Lots of people in our culture have similar feelings: They know or hope or suspect that certain things will happen to them. Do you have any ideas about this? Vague ideas or specific ones? Things you might have learned from your parents when you were a little girl?"

"Nothing," Joanne said sullenly, turning her face to the wall. "When you go you go, that's all. And you're all alone. No one can help you through it."

"Is it the aloneness that bothers you?" I asked her.

"Of *course* it's the aloneness," she said with sudden energy. "What could be lonelier than being without your family?" Joanne, I had been told, had always been a busy, gregarious woman, and she had valued personal relationships above all else.

A couple of sessions later, Joanne told me in a musing voice, "You know, I would really like to see my father again. I'd like to see him the way he used to be, not the way I see him in my mind ever since he died." I knew from earlier sessions that her father had died during a violent epileptic seizure, which Joanne, at age ten, had witnessed. This was an image that never left her.

Finally shown a path to try, I responded, "Reunion with loved ones after death is a notion that comes up all over the world. Many people in this country who have experienced near-death experiences report reunions with their deceased loved ones. And cultures all over the world describe meeting ancestors beyond death. They say reunions are possible, Joanne," I said, hoping she would share with me the possibility that perhaps she would see her father again. "Would you like to read about it?" I asked.

No hesitation: "Yes."

Joanne had been a voracious reader all her life, though she'd quit reading when her doctors said they could do no more for her. Now she began to read widely on the subject of reunion. Soon she began to initiate conversations about her own preparations for death, confessing sheepishly to a secret: She was looking forward to it—well, not to death itself but certainly to seeing her father once more. Soothed by the concept of reunion, she acquainted herself with death, and that familiarity soon allowed her to take care of her unfinished business. She made her will, talked extensively with her friends and children about their lives after her death, and implied, if not promised, that she would see them again.

THE VALUE AND POWER OF STORIES

Extensive literature searches have revealed a distinct scarcity of studies designed to prove that exposure to ideas and images of the afterdeath actually brings benefits to the seeker. More such empirical research would be welcome, and given the changing environment in science, where old prejudices are giving way to a new openness to possibilities, I hope that such work is not far off. In that vein, the Dalai Lama, spiritual leader of Tibetan Buddhism, has offered a substantial reward to anyone who can prove there is *not* an afterdeath—an imaginative variation on the more usual, and more cynical, view that dares the proponent to provide proof.

In this book, I employ what is known as the natural history approach to science, an approach analogous to the methods employed by basic scientists who collect specimens as fodder for their eventual theories. In the case of afterdeath research, the specimens are not rocks or animals but human beliefs and experiences. By collecting "samples" of afterdeath beliefs and experiences, we—like those who employed this method before us—can lay a basis for further study of this new field of the afterdeath. Throughout this book I will offer samples both of the diverse ways other cultures see the afterdeath experience and experiences of clients in my practice who have grappled in my presence with their expectations of imminent death. I will describe cases as well where principles and anecdotes of the afterdeath have psychological meaning to patients and profound assistance in the healing process in general.

These examples and anecdotes are presented not as scientific proof of the power of the world's wisdom, but rather as illustrations of ways in which images and ideas of the afterdeath can break rigid habits of being and open the doors of possibility. If we approach these perspectives not as scientists but as seekers, trying out first this new light, then that strange idea, the mysteries and puzzles that have remained so stubbornly in the shadows may begin to gain definition. As evidence that this is so, I conclude this chapter with a personal anecdote that, in its quiet way, dramatizes the approach I have described.

In the late 1980s, I traveled with my colleague Edmundo Barbosa to Sulawesi, Indonesia. Edmundo, a colleague who works with cancer patients and is a student of Brazilian rituals, has traveled extensively with me and has taught me a great deal about preparing to encounter disparate ways of thinking. We journeyed to Indonesia to collect afterdeath data.

In Sulawesi, when a child dies it is buried, not in the earth, but in the carved-out trunk of a beautiful tree surrounded by a ring of benches. On a mild day, Edmundo and I sat together below this massive tree and looked up at the trunk with its little carved niches in which the small coffins go. As the tree grows, we were told, the child is taken closer to the heavens and to God.

We sat silently on the bench under the boughs of this magnificent tree, and what came to me was a profound respect. I felt I was witnessing something of such beauty, of such great compassion, that I became very, very quiet. I started to think of children who had died, the pain those deaths had caused, and the severity of those losses. It was lovely for me to learn that children had been buried in the tree in order to be constantly moved toward the sky. I spent a lot of time looking first at the tree and then at the sky, the tree and then the sky.

I thought of the tree not only as the physical bearer of the children but also as their perpetuator. The leaves, the roots, the seasons affecting the tree and its renewal—all these were imbued with the spirits of the children buried in its trunk. Into my mind came the prayer flags of Tibet—handmade pieces of colorful cloth inscribed with messages and hung on wires on almost every house. The Tibetans hang these flags around their homes so that the winds will spread the prayers or greetings written on them throughout the world. The tree, I reflected, was doing the same with these children: spreading their spirits into the air around us and who knows where else.

The entire experience reminded me of a poem by Chinese poet Li Po that I looked up later:

> *The birds have vanished into the sky,*
> *and now the last cloud drains away.*
>
> *We sit together, the mountain and me,*
> *until only the mountain remains.*[2]

When adults die in Sulawesi, whenever their family is able to attain twenty-four water buffalo to make the required sacrifice, effigies called *tau-tau* are made of the dead person. A *tau-tau* is a wooden doll about three feet high. Its right hand is extended palm sideways to receive a blessing from above; the left hand is extended palm upward to pass on the blessings to the community. The *tau-tau* is placed with crowds and crowds of other *tau-taus* in caves, carved niches, or mountains above and surrounding the community. They look down on and watch over the community at all times, and just above and beside the *tau-taus* are the actual graves, or holes dug into the mountainside, where the bodies of the dead are buried.

To me, the authenticity of the comfort the *tau-tau* affords is unquestionable. As the children's tree focused our attention on the beauty and dependability of nature, so the effigies of the adult dead brought subtle, complex pleasures of art to the community. Could the devastating emotions of loss and abandonment be softened with a more comforting effect than the artist's effort to render a spirit and a body as it was in life—familiar, comfortable, and now watching over the community as a bridge between the living and dead?

When I first saw the *tau-tau* of the Sulawesi, I wished that my friend James had allowed his apartment to be filled to bursting with images of the afterdeath. I own many pieces of skeleton art from Mexico, one of which is of a man sitting in a bathtub, naked. He is a skeleton smoking a cigarette and musing, just as James used to do. Among my collection of beautiful Day of the Dead sculptures from Mexico are some tall women, elegantly dressed as James liked women to be— proper purses and looking coyly at the viewer, hats jauntily perched, inviting. Except that they are skeletons. Familiar figures, but dead.

Had death become even somewhat normal to James—had he lived with it through art on a daily basis—perhaps today his own image might be living in the memories of his friends with a relaxed and accepting smile on his face instead of the expression of deep anxiety with which he faced his last weeks. Simply living with such art and imagery might have opened him to the chance that there was more to the mystery of existence than he could see or taste or feel as he lay on his deathbed in terror.

CHAPTER 2

ℐℐℐ

Crossing Borders Within and Without

Everyone may educate and regulate his imagination so as to come thereby into contact with spirits, and be taught by them.

—Paracelsus

Through my work, art, data, and its supporting literature poured into my life. But in the end, research and reflection are no substitute for experience. At many points during my ongoing collecting, I suddenly found myself with the yen to travel and learn for myself what the people in faraway places I was studying might see. One day as I worked in my apartment in New York surrounded by stacks of books on death and the afterdeath, I called my colleague Edmundo Barbosa. It was a call that would ultimately lead me to a mystery within myself. This was the vital imagination, the conduit in the psyche to unseen aspects of reality, of which the afterdeath was perhaps the most compelling.

"Look, I'm bored with my reading again," I told Edmundo on the phone. "I can't pick this stuff up only off the page, I've got to experience it. I want to go back to Brazil. It's time to take a trip."

"Journey, not trip," he corrected me, making a distinction he had made many times before. Then my dependable magic tour guide half spoke, half sighed. "Ah, Sukie," he said through the international phone wire, followed by a single word: "Candomble."

I hadn't done all that reading and note taking for nothing. I knew what he meant. Besides, we had discussed Candomble many times as the ultimate goal of Brazilian research. This was an Afro-Brazilian religion originating in West Africa that had found a way to hide itself in the rich folds of the garments of Brazilian Catholicism. Deep within the skirts and ruffles of the Catholic Church lived—and I do mean *lived,* with a secret, irrepressible vitality—a panoply of saints and gods that the pope and his bishops had never heard of.

Even for the most devout Brazilians, the spirit world of Candomble is not easy to enter. A seven-year initiation precedes the moment when, with shaved head, an initiate yields to the call of an Orisa—a particular, personalized god—and dances into an altered state during which the Orisa climbs onto the person, rides, and directs. It is called incorporation.

A year earlier, Edmundo had taken me to an evening-long Candomble ritual in Brazil, and I had found myself transported, by the incessant drumming, out of my Western skepticism and natural fear of migraine into a state in which all aspects of life were brightened, lightened, charged with electricity. Xango, the God of thunder and fire, to whom the evening was dedicated, did indeed arrive on the scene, and nobody could have escaped the excitement of his arrival.

But I had never been to the heart of Candomble, where the dead— the Egun—live. I knew through my research and the strange half-gossipy, half-scholarly trail Edmundo had been guiding me along in Brazil for several years since I'd met him there each September, on a small island off the coast of northern Brazil, that the Egun appeared to the living in a forty-eight-hour ritual of the Return of the Dead. When Edmundo spoke that word "Candomble" into the phone, I knew he meant it was time for us to travel to the heart of the matter. For years we had been painstakingly following the threads that crossed the boundaries and even wove together the worlds of the living and dead. It seemed that now was the time to plunge from one to another, to meet the Egun on their yearly return.

The journey was hellish. Everything went wrong. As I landed in

Rio, President Bush declared the beginning of Desert Storm, and the focus of the whole world shifted to the bleak Kuwaiti desert and the fear of terrorism. As a result of the heightened security, my luggage was lost. Lost also were our Candomble contacts—long cultivated, dearly protected: All had somehow sustained sudden accidents and were unable to accompany us. Things went wrong at our hotel, too. Both Edmundo and I became ill; it rained steadily every day, every hour; and everything conspired against our finding and then reaching the island off the coast where the dead would return to the living.

"But you understand, Sukie," said my urbane colleague, "one does not simply walk into the afterdeath. The journey itself is part of a barrier between worlds. Patience, patience. We will arrive. Or we will not."

Typically Brazilian in his ambiguity: reassuring, and not.

All our plans failed, but by a series of extraordinary coincidences we managed to find transport to the island. Once there we sought the chief as we had been directed. We had been told that it was critical that we find him and introduce ourselves, since he would not know that we, strangers and foreigners, were coming. I was apprehensive, but the chief, a huge man, received us open-armed, saying, "We have been expecting you. They are awaiting you on the *terreiroi*."

"The sacred ground," Edmundo translated for me, whispering, his face showing that he, too, was thinking as I was, that perhaps the chief in his unexpected expansiveness had us confused with someone else.

The chief led us to a cottage without a floor, inner walls, furniture, or a bathroom, but clearly a place of honor only twenty feet from the temple itself. "Don't leave," he warned. "The Egun are all around us, as are the Aparaca—tall ghosts in limbo who shriek out their misery. Be careful! Careful! Walk only with an initiate. We will come and get you when it is time."

At sundown, in our little house, I wondered at the wisdom of coming here. We were trapped on sacred ground with no floor, no bathroom, and no friends. I chided myself. It was typical of these trips for me to become so engrossed in the strategies of getting to a place that I gave little thought to whether it made more sense to stay home. This night, still ill and without even the amenities of walls to afford privacy, I didn't have to wonder. Warnings we had received and that I had taken in stride with my New York bravado—"Do not share your water with anyone! They will want your water," and "Avoid all blood sacrifices! They will want *you* to make a blood sacrifice!"—suddenly came back to haunt me. The sheer eeriness of what we were doing in tracking shadowy images of the dead wouldn't leave me. I was sick, tired, far from home, on a mountaintop on an island—and on sacred ground with no discernible exit.

But time to worry was short. The sun set, the stars began to shimmer, and initiates came to sweep us into the hot, crowded, urine-smelling temple, where there were two lime-filled bathrooms—one for men, one for women (the ritual would last forty-eight hours)—and where nonstop drumming was already going on. Babies were passed overhead from hand to hand the moment they fretted—though when they reached me, which they did every so often where I stood on the women's side of the room, they would mortify me by bursting out wailing. The drums changed rhythm as two young men were initiated, covered in the blood and feathers of the live chickens that the chief had waved throughout the room moments before.

Overwhelmed by the sheer lack of anything familiar within the temple—Edmundo was on the men's side and hidden from my view by a pillar—I focused my concern on the children. To be sure, the babies were kept safely in the women's section, but the older children were together, alone, with no parental supervision right up in front where the rituals were taking place. They seemed to be having a grand old time, but I worried: What are the children doing here at the Return of the Dead?

The drumming was pounding in my head. The smell of blood mingled with the odor of urine and sweat. The human heat, building fast, made me long for our floorless shelter.

Suddenly the locked double doors at the back of the temple flew open and something magnificent rushed in! A whirling, twirling headlessness in a robe—a robe the many colors of Joseph's, a robe, I was told, that would burn you if you touched it—flew singing and rumbling and chanting through the white-dressed initiates, dodging and pirouetting up to the front.

It was an Egun, an Ancestor, a Dead. And it was glorious!

I stood, mouth open and spontaneous tears streaming down my face, watching the children, who immediately stood up and began singing and clapping out what appeared to be a welcoming song. A thrilling tension built between the Egun and the crowd in the hall as the initiates began to chase the spirit with special sticks, pounding them on the floor to make rhythmic taps and filling the room with a beautiful pandemonium that drowned out the drumming. Chased in a fashion that reminded me somewhat of the Keystone Kops, the Egun disappeared, ran back into the night—but no sooner was it gone than another whirled in. All night the most beautiful and magnificent creatures—magical, colorful, graceful, headless dancing creatures—spun through the hall and elicited the rhythms of people's clapping hands and clacking sticks. My reticence, my nervousness, my resistance to the heat and smells and sounds had all flown away with the appearance of the first Egun. Transported into the afterdeath, I was having as exciting and wonderful a time that night as I ever experienced anywhere.

For years I had been working, reading, traveling, interviewing, collecting, and integrating data. On the night of the Return of the Dead, the dependable boundaries in my mind between the real and unreal, fact and fiction, perception and hallucination disintegrated under the bombardment of sounds, sights, odors, colors, and rhythms. Suddenly, through the force of my own vital imagination—a force I shared with the strangers on that island but had never to such a conscious degree experienced in my life in New York—I was mingling with the living and the dead. Bouncing between wonder and joy, I clapped and laughed with the others, delighting with them at the return of the magnificent, colorful, formidable, incredibly vital, energetic dead.

At dawn, with cracks of light penetrating the tightly shuttered windows and doors of the temple, the crowd moved slowly outside. The sun was beginning to rise as the moon began to set. Both hung in the sky and the air was sweet and cool. Someone told us to wait—something special was about to happen.

What more wonderful things could take place? I wondered, but then I saw. Gathered in the meadow below us were all the Egun together at once. I counted sixteen, but they continued to dance and swirl, so I'm not really sure of the number. Now I noticed that little mirrors were embedded in their twirling robes that caught the light and threw it back to us. The initiates surrounded the Egun at intervals, alert, their sticks pounding, to enforce the line between the living and dead. Then an Egun got away! He was the newest one, someone told me, and still very frisky. (All Egun are male—when women die, they return to nature as do most men. Only some men go on to become ancestors.) Puppylike, the new Egun ran and skipped toward the crowd with the little bells on his robe ringing, obviously very pleased with himself. This Egun ran fast, but so did the initiates, and they cornered him at last before he reached the crowd and escorted him back down the little hill to the meadow to join the others. All the Egun danced and marched away behind the temple. The sun was fully up now and the moon had disappeared.

The ritual went on for another day. A goat we had seen at the entrance to the *terreiroi* was assisted into the afterdeath and cooked and distributed in a grand picnic lunch. Then there was time for talk, rest, and reflection along with digestion before the initiates arrived again, and we entered the temple for another night of reunion.

After forty-eight hours on the island, Edmundo and I, dazed by the experience, returned to the mainland, and then I flew home. For years we tried, unsuccessfully, to go back. But wherever I went I carried with me memories of those two extraordinary days.

Five years later, after much travel, particularly in the East, collecting information and images of the afterdeath, I returned home from a trip with a raging virus. I was miserably ill. I arrived in New York with a 103-degree fever and the whole known array of what I took to be flu symptoms. But the night of comfort in my own bed I had obsessively imagined throughout the long flight home was not to be—at least not quite yet. I returned to discover that my mother was deathly ill and had to be hospitalized. As a doctor's daughter I knew all the right things to do and did them, all the while shaking and trembling with fever. But once my chronically ill eighty-one-year-old mother was admitted into the hospital, she suffered a heart attack. Her immediate future looked very problematic.

My flu prevailed as did my mother's reactivated tuberculosis, so the bedside vigil I intended and wanted very much to keep was not to be. I was infectious and was sent away. I had to go home and go to bed. Finally, I could collapse.

I filled the tub and soaked in my bath. Then I shook and cramped my way into bed. I sank down beneath the covers, each lovely detail of which I had imagined on the plane. Sleep, beautiful sleep, gradually overtook me, and I drifted.

I woke to a drumming. I dragged myself upright and listened.

Drumming. That damn kid next door, I concluded, and roused myself to pound on our shared wall. As my fist was about to meet the wall, I listened more carefully. The drumming was in my living room, and furthermore, I *knew* that drumming. It was the drumming I had heard on the island on the night of the Return of the Dead. It wasn't coming from next door. It was in my living room.

Confused as to who had invaded my apartment, I forced myself out of bed and toward the sound of the drums.

In the living room I found everyone, *everyone,* living *and* dead, who had filled the hall on that faraway island—now dancing and welcoming me in my own home. Everyone had come and everyone smiled—as if we had always met this way and as if each person in the community was very glad to see me. No one spoke, everyone smiled, and the drummers drummed.

Luis was there, a man who had befriended us during our time on the island and spoken of the Aparaca, miserable shrieking ghosts who accompany the arrival of the Egun. He was dressed in the whites of the initiate, his stick in his hand ready to ward off the ghosts that made the eerie sounds and to physically maintain the boundary between the living and the dead.

Christina was in my kitchen cooking for the assembled, just as she had done on the island, and a magnificent odor of I have no idea what came drifting toward me as I stood astonished.

Another familiar face smiled up at me from a chair; still another face gazed from next to my bookcase. Beer was flowing liberally (I don't keep beer), I could hear the toilet flushing, and children played tag around the coffee table. Everywhere were people I remembered. "Everything, it will be all right," said Luciano, who had visited Edmundo and me in our wall-less house and talked with us there for a long time. He had told us that the Egun had appeared at his baptism and run off with him, to the consternation of those gathered in the temple to witness the ceremony. Later, a senior researcher explained to us that Luciano had been a very sick little baby and that the Egun had taken him away to cure him.

Sergio gave me the first of the food prepared in my kitchen, but the crowd, the smoke, the sweet odor filling my living room became too much for me, and suddenly I rushed out. An intense, colorful, headless, muttering figure followed me—an Egun! I was careful not to let his robes touch me. I stopped, deeply honored, overwhelmed with gratitude at his visit.

"Sukie, you're hallucinating," said I, the surgeon's daughter, psychotherapist, and New York skeptic as I bowed to this most magical and foreign entity. "Go back to bed, take some aspirin, and go to sleep."

In the midst of this commotion Edmundo called—it was six A.M. in Brazil. His wife had had a miscarriage.

Then the hospital called. My mother had had a second heart attack. Still banished from her bedside, I returned sadly to bed.

Still the drums persisted, and I noticed that, against all odds and for no accountable reason, I was calm—and the feeling of being honored and comforted by the presence of the exotic creatures from the other side of life in my living room would not leave me.

Questions floated through my mind as I lay down and began to drift to the drums:

- Was my mother, who was about to die, also about to disappear? The answer came as concrete as the colorful figures in the crowd on the other side of the wall. Hardly, I thought, she would simply "cross over," and perhaps not so impermanently.
- If I were to take a sudden turn for the worse and begin to court

death—such ideas occur to a doctor's daughter when tempera-
tures rise steeply—would that be such a tragedy? Here too my
attitude toward death seemed softened and tempered by the rich
blend of interacting, interweaving living and dead currently in-
habiting my living room while the heat of my fever was burning
away the orderly boundaries between life and death.

What on earth happened in my apartment that night? Was I dreaming? Fantasizing? Hallucinating? There is an answer: I was imagining.
But not in the way we are used to understanding and using that term
to refer to a slightly childish, vaguely useless pursuit akin to day-
dreaming. Rather, the extreme conditions of my life that night—
exhaustion, high fever, unrelenting anxiety regarding my mother—
combined into a classic trigger for my vital imagination, the capacity
of my psyche not merely to visualize but to experience another realm
of reality.

My research had accustomed me to the idea that a large proportion
of the world's people can access other realms: reports brought back by
shamans, descriptions embedded in the culture, mental maps of the
afterdeath geography, and accounts of the inhabitants there—these
are all integrated without awe into daily life. For many people of the
world, realms after death are as indisputably there as San Francisco is
to New Yorkers, as Africa is to Brazilians. It is a case of living within
the whole of reality, not just the parts one can see.

Many in the West have written of such realms, and a growing body
of literature not only poses the existence of other aspects of reality but
minutely studies the rare but powerful capacity to apprehend them.
"The voyage of discovery lies not in seeking new vistas but in having
new eyes," wrote Marcel Proust, emphasizing the focus on *how* we
reach exotic realms rather than the realms themselves.

At the center of these investigations lies the work of French Islamic
mystic and scholar Henry Corbin. Corbin made the now classic distinction between an imagined realm and what he called an *imaginal*
one. The former might be the Egun as you, the reader, apprehended
them in your mind in response to my description of them. The *imaginal* realm is a real world, apprehended not by the five usual senses

alone but by a highly sensitized, transformed imagination that functions in and of itself as an organ of perception.[1] In other words, not fantasy, not dreaming, not hallucination, but the perception of an aspect of a greater reality not ordinarily seen.

Many have responded to Corbin's ideas, developed them further, and related them to their own innovative work. Most suggest that this capacity to apprehend the hidden is identical to the powers of the shamans of tribal cultures—after intense training—to cross the borders limiting ordinary experience. Some, in particular Kenneth Ring, also link this crossing over into another aspect of existence to the experiences reported by those who have had near-death experiences.[2] That is, the apprehension of a great light, the tunnel, and the reunion with loved ones is to these writers the same kind of experience as that of shamans who transcend the ordinary and enter the invisible—although the content they find there is not necessarily the same at all.

The hard sciences have shown equal interest in the imaginal world, at least along their more radical borders. Physicist Michael Talbot speaks to the work of Corbin in his book *The Holographic Universe,*[3] calling it the land of nowhere, and physicist Fred Alan Wolf uses the concept of the imaginal as well in his book *The Dreaming Universe.*[4]

Other links in Western writing, too, identify visionary experience with this extraordinary capacity for perception. Samuel Taylor Coleridge and William Blake are two poets who have contributed to our Western canon of literature detailed images from other worlds, worlds hidden by reality as we ordinarily perceive it. In contexts both spiritual and adventurous, certain psychedelic drug experiences suggest an identical breakthrough: Terence McKenna, of whom I write later in this book, describes psychopharmacological episodes as findings from the afterdeath.

All these disparate descriptions describe ways into—or over, or behind, or through—ordinary reality. Most significant, though, is not where the extraordinary realm lies but *that* it lies: It is real, it has form and dimension, and above all it is inhabited.

Those I encountered in the imaginal realm on the night my mother was dying were the Egun. Both my ability to see them and their presence itself were aspects of the vital imagination.

For many tribal peoples of the world, hidden realms are as real and ultimately reachable as a destination on an airline schedule. They may be invisible but they are nevertheless a known part of the whole and taken for granted as such. This tells us that it is not necessary to be a shaman, a Near Death Experiencer, or a particularly gifted individual to experience the vital imagination. I want to suggest that such a capacity to apprehend the extraordinary exists universally in all human beings. The vital imagination is both tool and goal. We draw on this capacity both within ourselves and to reach into other realms. This most difficult and elusive of concepts jumps boundaries. It is neither this nor that, it is both: the vessel and its contents; the airplane and the destination; the hammer, the nails, and the house. Its effects, both in us and around us, are incredibly powerful.

So what *was* going on in my living room that night?

I have no doubt: My vital imagination had been triggered, and I had broken through the normal bonds of perception. Most accounts of such breakthroughs describe them as resulting from extreme conditions that serve as stimuli. For shamans and mystics, and those seeking mystical experiences, such conditions are often rituals designed to provide extraordinary perceptions. For other kinds of seekers the triggers can be psychedelic drugs. For those who cross the borders involuntarily, near-death or other traumas evoke the perceptions. For me, that night, it was the combustible combination of exhaustion, illness, and anxiety that induced my vital imagination. But there was more as well that contributed to its accessibility: I had a longing to know, a yearning to experience the unknown, the ambiguous, the mysterious. These yearnings sharpened my ability to approach the border.

The experiences that the vital imagination yields need not be so dramatic and extreme as my midnight visitation. There are moments of breakthrough as subtle and penetrating as a dance, as natural as the wind. The effects of these moments are immeasurable, but to brush them aside without appreciating their essence is to lose the touch of the extraordinary that they lend to everyday life.

Ruth

Ruth, a widow, was sixty-eight when we began our work together. She came to me when she was diagnosed with Chronic Lymphocytic Leukemia (CLL). As cancer goes, CLL progresses slowly, and Ruth's doctors told her it was most likely that at her age she would ultimately die of something else. But CLL is not an easy thing to live with: Ruth's skin became thin and bled easily, and over the course of several years she lost vitality and was treated with many toxic drugs. Ultimately she required frequent blood transfusions.

Ruth had never been sick before, and she found it emotionally painful and very frightening. She came from a family that blamed people for their illness and believed that all disease was caused by not taking proper care of yourself. Ruth had taken great pride in her ability to take good care of herself. It had been her safety net. To her, illness was almost a moral weakness, which added to her suffering.

Ruth was frequently mistaken for someone younger than her age and had always been proud of her appearance and her vitality. Now, under the onslaught of illness, she looked older than her peers. For the first time it occurred to her that she might grow old. She was devastated and deeply frightened. So she came to therapy.

Ruth did everything possible to hold on to life as it had been before her diagnosis. As the years went by, her occasional transfusions became more frequent and her skin bled so easily that her clothing was often bloodstained where a seam had rubbed against it. Still, she persisted in living her life as usual—going to the theater or the ballet, seeing friends, shopping, cooking, and entertaining as she had done all her adult life. She fought at all costs to be "normal," to be in control of her appearance and her life. Anything else was unthinkable. As she fought to maintain her normalcy, she consequently became more and more rigid in her ways.

Our sessions were basically supportive. We appeared to be more like friends chatting than client and psychotherapist seeking occasions of deep insight, experience, or revelation. Ruth did not examine her life in depth; nor was it easy for her to trust others. Eventually, after I had listened for many hours to her reports of her daily life, I became the friend she had never had, the one who could be trusted, and we fell into an undeviating routine. Ruth would come to see me every week, between her hair appointment and her dinner with "the girls," and I listened attentively as she moved from subject to subject across the surface of her life.

Then one day, after many years of this routine, Ruth called for an extra appointment—something she had never done before. I was very curious: What could bring Ruth to a second appointment in one week? I soon learned that it was an experience of the vital imagination.

Ruth had gone to the post office to mail some letters, and as she waited in line "everything changed." As she described it, "A strong feeling came over me, and suddenly all the people there lost their faces and their distinctive clothing and became the same, like blobs. I was weak from not having eaten yet for the day. I had just taken a new medicine that needed to be taken on an empty stomach and I felt so strange that I left my place in line and leaned against a wall. I had a view of the entire huge post office—it's one of the bigger ones—and as I rested there, things did not go back to normal as I had expected them to. Instead the people—or should I say blobs—I could see were all in some way connected. Their movements were connected in a sort of ballet, but it was a balanced ballet."

"What is a balanced ballet?" I asked, fascinated.

In the most matter-of-fact way, she told me that when one person—or blob person—made a movement on one side of the floor, someone else on the other side of the room made a perfectly reciprocal movement.

"As I watched," said Ruth, "I saw that there really were no random motions, no motions that were not responded to by other motions. The entire post office was aglow, in motion, connected as if moving to some music I couldn't hear. Someone would leave a line, and someone, somewhere else in the post office, would join a line; someone would leave the building, and someone else would step in; a clerk would rudely ignore someone, and another clerk would lean toward someone else in a helpful way. Throughout, there was the occasional sound of the machines stamp-pounding pieces of mail. Whenever that would happen, everyone, for the tiniest second—and I could *see* that tiny second—would pause in their movements and then go on. I thought that perhaps I had gone crazy and that I would never get out of there. Then someone—a blob person—leaning against the opposite wall waved to me, and I knew I would be all right. What happened, Sukie? Am I all right?"

I listened, surprised and entranced. Of all my patients, Ruth was the least likely I would have thought to have had a breakthrough out of her contained, controlled consciousness. After some discussion, Ruth remembered again the new drug and immediately assigned it a causal role.

She both asked and stated: "It was the drug, right? I was drugged," a formulation that appealed to her sense of normalcy. Everyone knows drugs can make you dizzy, or even crazy.

"Yes," I answered, "I do think it was the drug, but not in the way you think it was. Perhaps the drug was the occasion but not the cause of what happened. I think that the drug made possible the experience."

Michael Murphy, who wrote the book *The Transformation of the Body*, speaks of the "imagination with hands that can part curtains."[5] Using this image, I explained the vital imagination to Ruth.

"Then it was real? I experienced something *real?*"

"You had the experience, didn't you?" I responded.

"Yes," she said pensively. "I certainly did. I even went back the next day, but the post office was itself again: smelly, dirty, filled with bums and rude people—the usual. I couldn't believe that the day before it had been an exquisite ballet."

"The day before," I said, "the vital imagination had parted the curtains for you. The next time, everything was back to normal. Your body had absorbed your new drug as part of your daily routine—and had become the usual. I would say usual rather than normal," I attempted. "Normal is really too hard to define these days."

"Hmm," she said musing, and our time was up.

Over the next years, Ruth became less "normal." She did not mention the experience again but she did not forget it and, like others who have had experiences of and through the vital imagination, she was never quite the same. She became interested first in off-Broadway and then in off-off-Broadway and then even in performance art. She began to cultivate friends who were creative, as she explained it—artists and designers—and she grew less rigid and less frightened. Eventually she died, in a state of expectation, she told me, as to where her vital imagination would lead her next.

There is more than enrichment to be had from the gifts of the vital imagination. It appears that lessons, information, answers—all are possible, though not guaranteed, to those who even momentarily cross the border.

Norman

Norman, a physician client of mine, told me the following story when he returned to New York at Christmas and we had a catch-up session. He had moved to California to take a faculty position at the Stanford School of Medicine and found himself thrilled with the wildness and lush greenness of the miles of open land between the school and the ocean. Not yet having developed any friends with whom to spend time, he had driven into the mountains one Saturday, parked his car beside the winding two-lane road, and simply walked off into the woods alone. He smiled and shook his head in amazement as he told the story. We agreed that only a New Yorker would ever do such a thing. But New Yorker that he was, he walked for hours, wearing only a light jacket. Suddenly Norman noticed that the day was waning, and he had begun to grow cold. He turned then to go back to his car, but after walking for some time realized that the land was completely unfamiliar . . . he didn't know the way back to the road.

Turning again, he began walking through the forest the other way, hoping to find something he had seen before and unwilling to admit that he was lost. As time went on he became more and more frightened. He had told no one where he was going; he had not known anyone to tell. He was lost for sure. It was growing dark, and he had become tired. In a last effort, he began to climb upward, struggling to the top of the thickly forested ridge and shouting occasionally, but hearing no sound at all except the beating of his own heart. Suddenly he crested the ridge and found himself standing on the lip of a thickly forested bowl-shaped valley. Beyond the rim of the valley, the sun was sinking. He stood there for some time, sweating, exhausted, and terrified, cursing himself for his stupidity.

Then it happened.

"Suddenly, I wasn't alone. I became intensely aware of the thousands and thousands of trees around me. Their forms gradually dissolved until I could see what I call their 'life force.' They were no longer just trees but were undulating, vibrating, making a sound as if they were humming. They were still trees but something more as well.

"A peacefulness fell upon me and I decided to sit beneath one of these wondrous things. We all watched together as the sun sank behind the ridge. I was stunned by what I was feeling and, doc that I am, checked for a bump on my head—maybe I had fallen down and didn't remember, or blood in my hair—maybe I was suffering a concussion. But there was no bump, no blood, and even my pulse was normal.

"After a while, a sort of wind came up, and we all swayed to it, naturally. It was like, what else is there to do in a wind? The swaying showed me that there was a kind of natural direction flowing through us all, and I began to move deliberately in that direction. For no earthly reason, I felt a great certainty that I was now going in the right direction, and I continued to move on—without fear, even though it got dark. Eventually I stepped out of the forest onto the road. When I looked behind me the trees were as they once had been, big, leafy, green and emotionally distant."

"How amazing," I said and we sat in the dust-filled, light-filtered silence that surrounded us.

"And my car was parked about thirty yards to my right," he added as an afterthought.

Norman knew that he had not imagined but had rather experienced something. As so many others have described it, for a brief time he felt himself to be "someplace else," outside time and space as he had previously known it. He put it this way: "It was as if I had gained access to the hidden life around me."

. . .

When the vital imagination enables us to experience the afterdeath, we share with others who have also done so. This access and the realms reached can render a sense of comfort in the face of death. The experience of the vital imagination has brought to many throughout the world a confirmation that energy can exist beyond the border of life and death. This contradicts the fear that all might simply disappear when life as we know it ends. In those cultures where the vital imagination functions most freely, death is not necessarily a source of terror. People do not dread it, and they often die in ways that are more interactive, compassionate, and healing than that of the now classic Western model—a technological nightmare played out in a hospital room.

In Mexico on the annual celebration called the Day of the Dead, the living picnic and even party in graveyards with their dead family members and friends. The ongoing nature of life after death is portrayed with humor and whimsy in the small clay figures of skeletons one sees everywhere. The skeletons—some with eyeglasses, some with hair, some chubby, some thin—are engaged in such mundane tasks as cooking, bathing, putting on makeup, or playing sports. Figures we might see as grotesque or suitable only for Halloween are permanent parts of the decor in homes.

It is similar in many Hindu houses in India. One commonly finds there paintings and sculptures of Kali, the goddess whose unique and close relationship with death is reflected in her horrific face, her pendulous breasts, and her necklace of bloody human skulls. Such art work would have no place in the contemporary American home. Yet the opportunity to confront such images—gifts of the vital imagination—allows a familiarity with the otherwise unknown. There is comfort and the potential for strength in the exposure. It is therefore not surprising that to many Hindus Kali is one of the most beloved of the gods.

The vital imagination has brought us other examples of death and the afterdeath. They abound. One of my favorite comes from Northern Japan. At two prescribed times a year it is generally believed that children who have died pass through a valley strewn with white rocks, and as the children pass over them, these rocks are transformed into eggshells. The parents of the dead children gather on the departing side of the valley and consult with blind mediums who have come to guide the children through this final passage. (Children being children, dead or alive, they want to tarry, to play among the rocks rather than to move on to what is next.) The parents leave shoes, teddy bears, sweaters and other such items in the valley for their children, to comfort them and keep them warm. Years ago when I first read of this, I thought these items were symbolic, but since the visit of the Egun, I know them to be true gifts.

To understand and benefit from the images and ideas in this book, it is not a requirement to have experienced hidden realities through the vital imagination. Such experiences are rare, and the vast majority of us go through life without ever having any. Many, if not most, who picnic on the graves of loved ones in Mexico have not visited those buried there on the other side. Not every Hindu family with a picture of Kali in the house has actually encountered the goddess. In fact, although many people are exposed to such experiences—through rituals or drugs—such breakthroughs are not necessarily voluntary, and those who have them unexpectedly as Ruth and Norman did, as I did myself, are mystified by their occurrence and their meaning.

We are indebted to those who have had such extraordinary experiences, who have written of them and who have made them known, often widely known. The great bodies of spiritual and religious imagery, special stories, and mythology—these are the stuff of the vital imagination. The visionary poetry of Blake, Dante, and Coleridge enters the heart of these mysteries. Mystics and psychopharmacological explorers alike have recorded and described their experiences as well. All such literature is available to everyone, and by this means all of us can learn of hidden realms and benefit from the exposure, once removed, to the vital imagination. We can take their experiences as evidence of "something more," of "someplace else," and take comfort in the other realms their visions convey.

Is it really possible to use information from the vital imagination? Can myths, images, lore make a true difference?

Vern

At seventy-two, my client Vern was a highly successful jazz musician. He described himself as a man of action and "totally ready to die if it comes to that." But Vern entered therapy because he had been plagued for years by a recurring nightmare of monsters "screaming my death at me" while pushing him toward a grave already marked with a gravestone on which his name is carved.

In the daytime, Vern affected a nonchalance about his death and even a mastery of his life. But his dreaming self was not so blase about his sense of encroaching old age and death. He had been having his dream since he hit sixty-five, and his night terrors and resulting sleep deprivation were ruining the quality of his life.

At first Vern spoke little of the dream that had led him to my office, alluding to it only in terms of how tired he was, how difficult a task— any task—had become because he was so weary, how greatly he needed naps in the afternoon, and so on. When he did finally mention the dream itself, however, I asked him what he thought would happen to him after he died.

"Afterwards? Afterwards? I have no idea," he responded, implying that I had become some kind of simpleton. "It's *now* that I'm concerned with," he explained. "I just want to get some sleep."

I had something prepared for him, a photograph of a huge sculpture of the Tibetan god Yamantaka. In this classic image, Yamantaka stands victorious on top of an animal, which in turn is mounting a human. The god is phenomenally ugly and has the head of a beast himself.

"How would you feel about replacing one image for another?" I asked hopefully.

"He's worse than my nightmare," Vern retorted.

"He is a wisdom figure. Yama is the god of death and Yamantaka is the conqueror of the fear of death. He is not death itself but the fear of it. The Tibetans believe that if one were to spend time meditating upon

Yamantaka—studying him, becoming used to him, even becoming comfortable with him—one might overcome or transcend the fear of death and find peace of mind."

Vern was silent for a long time, in and of itself a remarkable change.

Then, in a quiet voice unlike his usual bantering one, he said, "You know, I lied to you. I'm actually terrified of dying."

"No kidding," I said, joking with him now, since I knew that Vern could take just so much seriousness. "You think you're the only one?"

During another long silence I hoped Vern was considering the profound isolation his fears had brought him, and I got lucky:

"You mean, other people fear death?" asked my most extroverted yet isolated client. "It's not such an unusual thing?"

"No, it's not unusual at all."

"And you think my fear of death is coming out in my dreams?"

"I think there's a chance of that, yes," I remarked, attempting to make rational what I knew was, for Vern, a somewhat bizarre discussion.

"So you want me to pay some attention to this strange Tibetan thing," he rightly concluded.

"Why not try?" I responded. "I think it's a useful distinction, between death and the fear of it. And this is a picture of the god who conquers that fear. Take the picture home, spend some time with it, see what happens," I recommended, and Vern nodded, stuffed the picture into his pocket, and abruptly launched into a very funny monologue about New York traffic.

Contemplating the god Yamantaka, the god of the fear of death, did help Vern. He found reassurance in the fact that an entire culture acknowledged the power of the fear of death and actually had a prescription for dealing with it. Vern's exposure to an image from an ancient culture from halfway around the world gave him the feeling that not only was he not alone in fearing death, but he might even be connected by that fear to others—many others. Fear of death wasn't so unusual after all, he realized. Though Vern never got into a rhythm of contemplating Yamantaka as a daily event, he benefited greatly from knowing that to the Tibetans the fear of death could be engaged. Vern's dreams became less frequent and then less powerful. Eventually he was able to sleep whole nights through during the majority of a week.

Through the vital imaginings of the people of the world, all of us can gain access to realms beyond borders. The following chapters describe the afterdeath journey and its four distinct and critical stages. It is a journey that many around the world have taken, tapped into, seen, reported and acted upon, and passed along to us.

An Igbo villager in scarring a dying Nigerian woman so that she might be identified when she returns as a newborn child, a Hindu man washing the corpse of his mother in the Ganges, a Mexican woman packing a basket for a picnic in a graveyard on the Day of the Dead, and a woman lying in a hospital in New York City learning that she is beyond treatment—all these people, all of us, have access to and can benefit from the vital imagination. In the vital imagination we have a common element within us that allows us to see what is beyond simple sense perception—the possibility of my father's explanations of someplace else.

PART II

— ⌁ —

EXPLORING THE MORE:

The Four Stages of the Afterdeath Journey

CHAPTER 3

cIp

Stage I: Waiting

A Waiting Place . . . Imagined

*She didn't actually feel the weight lift off, but suddenly she is free of it—
that terrible burden of her sick and pain-wracked body, which has been
heavy upon her for so long. Now she feels a growing lightness—she is a
lightness, and there is joy, relief, and a new interest in her surroundings all
mixed in together.*

*Ah. She has died. Of course. She has slipped across. By forcing her
attention backward through time, to only moments past, she can hear her
husband and daughter, very faintly, murmuring, crying quietly. In some
peculiar way, though she is out now, she can even feel them stroking her
arms in farewell.*

*She is not tired, but languid. Though she's terribly curious about where she
is, she feels she will have plenty of time to become acquainted with the
environment. The light is soft and gray, a delicious reprieve from the reflective
white light of her hospital room, which has forced her to keep her eyes closed
for many weeks or to squint painfully into the faces of her loved ones.*

*There are voices all around her, presences. Were she to make herself
alert, she might be able to see them. But she feels sure: There will be time
for that.*

*"Rest now," whisper the presences. "You have come from a long way
off. Just rest." She is not sure whether she hears their words or actually
feels them stroke the inside of her mind.*

*In all of this there is something familiar; even the pearly, soft light is
familiar.*

Then she realizes: Wherever she is, the experience is that of wrapping up in her quilt on her couch at the end of a long day. This has always been her treat to herself, the special reward she gave herself every late afternoon, and throughout her last hospital stay she had craved to be there in her living room, cried for the feeling sometimes. Can she actually have died and wound up on her soft, velvety couch, her quilt pulled snugly up to her chin? She senses that the question is nonsensical and that the caretaking beings want to draw the question away. "Just rest," they say, or think, to her. "Just be. Everything will be taken care of."

Ask many who fear death what it is precisely that scares them, and the answer is likely to be "the nothingness, the emptiness of it all."

Yet no religious or cultural system on earth describes the afterdeath as an amorphous blob, a nothing. Quite the opposite: These systems acknowledge and mitigate the disorienting, anxiety-producing effect of emptiness by rendering in more or less detail a definite *place* beyond death, complete with landscape, inhabitants, climate, colors, routes through it, its own pleasures and dangers . . . in short, the very opposite of the sudden nothingness that haunts those who fear there is no "more." The systems vary as greatly as belief systems vary on this side of the border, but in no case is the afterdeath vague.

In many afterdeath systems the first place described—the first "stop" after death takes place—is a Waiting Place. The journey through the afterdeath begins with the death of the body, but few of the world's stories characterize the trip as hard, fast, and demanding from the beginning. Those that do see the newly deceased as swooping through the cosmos on the backs of giant birds or thrust into the far reaches of the sky. In most accounts, however, the opposite is true. Dying is acknowledged to be a profound crossing into a new reality. The greatness of the changes that occur requires that there be a stopping, a waiting. In Brazil, for example, our Guarani Indian senior researcher described the crossing this way: "When a soul arrives near its destination, it must wait for Nhanderu to open the 'door.' This is a waiting or resting place. Also, when a soul succeeds in entering, it first goes into the *opy* [prayer house], then rests in a hammock, smokes a pipe, and receives a 'child' body."

The systems we tend to think of as the "simplest" are those that often do not have this calming anteroom into the afterdeath. In many cultures where the realms of death are tightly linked with everyday life, people who die simply slip into a world that is virtually identical with the one they have just left. It is this way for the Kadiweu Indians, a tiny tribe of barely more than a thousand people who live in the deep forest of the Mato Grosso area of Brazil. At one time—like the Egyptians—the Kadiweu buried their dead with all their belongings: adornments, weapons, and household goods. But the Kadiweu took this practice a step further. As great horsepeople, they buried their best horses and even their best grooms as well. They believed that when they died they would join a community identical to that they had just left and would again, naturally, need their horses as well as everything else.

In systems such as these, where the dead simply slip across, not only are the physical details of the afterdeath familiar, but the people are, too. Among the dead on the other side are those who have died relatively recently as well as revered ancestors—all with the habits of existing, thinking, and believing that the living have known all their lives. The utter familiarity of place and inhabitants counters the fear of the unknown, and the petrifying vision of nothingness is avoided. This very familiarity makes a prolonged adjustment period in a Waiting Place unnecessary. The newly dead simply slip across, but this doesn't mean that they all do so without resistance.

In more complex systems, images of the afterdeath are usually more exotic, differing dramatically from the known life and often requiring radical, if involuntary, adjustments on the part of the dead. Most often in these complicated systems, the afterdeath journey is reported as taking the dead toward a goal or even many different goals. Here are some examples of goals of the journey:

- a goal of reunion with loved ones, described in the near-death experience;
- a goal of reunion with God, as in Christianity;
- a goal of being rewarded with endless pleasures of heaven, as in Islam;
- a goal of escaping the burdens of this life, as in Hinduism;
- a goal of achieving a form of Nirvana—blissful integration with the whole—if not in this life then in death;

- a goal of returning to life in a higher, more comfortable caste or station, held by Hindus not yet close to escaping the Wheel of Life;
- and a goal of learning from one's mistakes in order to return to a high level of consciousness, as in the Baha'i religion and different forms of esotericism.

In these goal-oriented systems, the dead travel toward a destination. It is in these afterdeath landscapes that we find that most comforting of interims, the Waiting Place, where rest is possible, fear abates, and the traveler prepares for the trip.

SUMMERLAND: A PERSONALIZED WAITING PLACE

Certain highly developed versions of the afterdeath journey come to us from the esoteric belief systems. A particularly fascinating example is the work of Paul Beard, former president of the College of Psychic Studies of London and one of the chief documentarians of the esoteric movement. In his book *Living On,* Beard gives a detailed description of a Waiting Place just across the border from the living.

Pieced together from his own and his colleagues' countless "communications with the dead," Beard's description is of Summerland, the initial stop on the afterdeath journey. Summerland is above all a resting place—and how best to rest than to define for yourself where, of all possible choices, you would feel most comfortable? To afford the greatest repose, Summerland is the embodiment of whatever you wish it to be: a cabin by a lake from your childhood, a penthouse apartment overlooking New York City, a high mountain in the heart of Tibet. "So now a man's interior dreams are put to the test by being granted to him," writes Beard. "All his earth wishes come true, or so it seems. At first, all is wonder and delight. It seems he has indeed found himself. . . . Here an ordinary, decent man begins to feel at home on finding an environment seemingly similar to those he knew on earth, where he meets friends and relatives and even finds a replica of the house he desires."[1]

It's not hard to see the workings of the vital imagination in Summerland: Let the dying open to a Waiting Place that will give them the most comfort—in all its detail, in all its specificity—and that will be where they will find themselves initially when they die.

In Beard's conception, Summerland is both imagined and objectively real. It is Beard's belief, like Henry Corbin's regarding imaginal reality, that thoughts themselves become real: that imagination creates. These actual creations turn into what C. S. Leadbeater and Annie Besant, major voices in theosophic philosophy, called thought forms, the manifest actions of the energy of our ideas, feelings, concepts, and aspirations. Once we create these forms, they are both visible to us and have the capacity to complete us. But the reality of our thoughts does not end with their energy: Both Besant and Leadbeater describe specific thoughts or categories of thoughts as having particular colors, rates of vibration, and shape. "Each man travels through space enclosed within a case of his own building," they write. "Through this medium he looks out upon the world. . . ."[2]

It is the power of thoughts to become palpable and real, according to Beard, that enables the newly dead to create their own personally desirable Waiting Places. Summerland is every individual's most welcoming, comforting anteroom to the afterdeath, where the deceased can rest and wait for the changes necessary to permit the journey to continue.

A PLACE TO TRANSFORM

Rest, comfort, and a chance for fear to abate—all these are tantalizing benefits of the Waiting Places just beyond death. Imagining these sites (whether physical or otherwise) has the potential to calm the anxieties of both the dying and the caring witnesses to their passage. But these are not the only functions of the Waiting Place—and, from the point

of view of the traveler into the afterdeath, not even the most important.

In all systems with Waiting Places, transformation is the chief function to be performed here. In the Waiting Place the person who has
died sheds the accoutrements of the physical life—including, of
course, the body—and begins to change into spirit.

On the adventure into the realms beyond death, the physical body,
the emotions, the individual personality, and all the illusions that
allow us to agree with others on the "reality" of life as we know it
before death—all these qualities are impediments and must gradually
drop away. Paul Beard, in his description of Summerland, invokes a
classic archetypal image that symbolizes this transformation: the
metamorphosis of the caterpillar into the butterfly.

If in life we are caterpillars munching from leaf to leaf to sustain
ourselves, the chrysalis we enter when we die and lie dormant within
is our Waiting Place. There, gradually, the necessary changes to
our beings take place, and we emerge in the afterdeath as ephemeral
spirits no longer bound by time and space. For a person fearful
of dying or fearful for one who is dying, imagining the natural,
familiar metamorphosis of the caterpillar brings a sense of familiarity to the transformation process that suggests its place among
nature's cycles.

Paul Beard describes the transformation process as removing the
many robes we wear upon our spirits.[3] Transpersonal psychology has
its own way of describing the necessary transformation from physical
to spiritual being: The ego dies there and what remains is called the
Self. Although many practices anticipate this transformation in life, it
is in the Waiting Place that the dead one becomes spirit, Self, or Soul.

Let me pause to clarify the terminology a bit, since semantics
frequently obscures the similarities in systems that most assume to be
highly distinct. There are significant differences, but it's well worth
noting that all these systems attempt to describe the mysteries of the
human psyche and their place, their function, in a larger reality. What
is called Self in transpersonal psychology is the equivalent of the soul,
an ongoing and eternal entity, in a Christian context. This entity is
called the *Atman* by the Hindus, *Ancestor* in the African beliefs, the

Ka in the Egyptian system, the *hun* by the Chenece, the *nefresh* in Judaism.

The ego—and its container, the personality—is the achiever in life, functioning in the world of time, space, and other egos to master life's tasks, face its challenges, and undertake its struggles. By contrast, the Self, or Soul, or Atman, operates outside time and space and is the receptacle not of knowledge—which feeds the ego—but of wisdom. I favor the word *spirit* or *traveler* when referring to the entity that emerges after crossing over from life, and I use these words inter- changeably throughout this book.

In the Waiting Place, then, the unencumbered spirit emerges. Here, as some people describe the process, we become streamlined for the journey, divested of those qualities and functions that only had meaning—or seemed to have meaning—in life.

Candomble Vision

The excitement of being dead elevates a person to the category of spirit. This enthusiasm bursts into a superhuman power, en- abling this person to see the world as . . . God does, including the world of dreams. The lived life is shown as in a movie, reviving not only the faded past but also the present. The spirit sees all without eyes. The spirit is the vision itself. If we are not careful, he will see through our eyes.

—Candomble interviewee on the transformation into spirit, Brazil

---

NEWER VIEWS OF THE WAITING PLACE

The Waiting Place is a calm place, a place of transition. Some people who have had near-death experiences have reported waiting in a doctor's outer office or in a long line like that in a train station.

Suddenly they have "understood" that somewhere, someone or something had made a decision, and they could go no further, but had to return to their lives.

Perhaps the strangest and most dramatic depiction of all Waiting Places, however, comes to us from the Spiritists of Brazil, whose belief system is based on the ideas of Alan Kardec, European thinker. In their highly contemporary view of the afterdeath, the newly dead are transported by spaceship to what are best described as hospitals, but facilities notably lacking the atmosphere of trauma and distress that our hospitals have. For the dead, of course, health care for the body is irrelevant; instead, in these hospitals the dead are cleansed of their addictions to smoking, alcohol, and food. Yet these are not punitive places, just cleansing ones. Here, writes Hernani Andrade, senior researcher and noted Brazilian parapsychologist, the spirits "recover from traumas which proceeded their deaths. In these treatment and recovering centers . . . [they] go through a period of adaptation to the new way of life."[4] The wait while the ministrations are performed is described as calm and timely. The dead simply reside here until it is time to move on.

STEWARDS OF THE WAITING PLACE

A key characteristic of Waiting Places is that they are not so very remote, but rather—to the potential benefit of both the living and the dead—lie just across the border from the living. Shamans can go there and then return, with detailed descriptions and reassurances. An example comes from the Delaware Indians, whose Chief Elkhair reported this vision of the journey of the soul:

> He beheld a bird of monstrous size resting upon a mountain. It was toward this landmark that he was led by a spirit who undertook to conduct him as far as the soul of a living being could go. It was apparently to instruct him in the nature of the soul's pilgrimage after death that the revelation was given to him. . . . Beyond [the] moun-

tains of storms Elkhair could not pass. . . . While it was forbidden for him to approach nearer he could at least hear the voices of departed souls beyond enjoying their heavenly existence.[5]

Chief Elkhair's visit is instructional but, in another example, from the Goldi people of Siberia, a shaman actually takes a soul across to the other side. He traps the soul of a deceased person in a sacred pillow and then mounts a notched tree to see into the distance to preview his journey. Two spirits come to assist him, and the shaman, the assistants, and the soul set off on a special dogsled supplied with nourishing food. As soon as the travelers reach the afterworld—here conceived as the underworld—he leaves the soul with relatives and returns to the living, carrying gifts and greetings.[6]

Although the dead have indeed passed over, at this early stage just after death, the living can still participate to some extent in the dead's experience. Many rituals and behaviors that are frequently interpreted simply as the initial stages of mourning are really ways for the living to help shepherd the dead through the transformation they undergo in the Waiting Place, or at least to hover a little.

India's Hindu system of the afterdeath is one of the most complex and detailed examples of the living shepherding the dead through their transformation. Here the loved ones entrust the well-being of the dead person in the Waiting Place to specialists known as Mahapatra, considered to be Untouchables, India's lowest social rank. The work of these specialists is to care for the corpse in a complex and ritualized manner in order to facilitate the natural transformation that is to take place.

When a faithful Hindu dies, or appears to be close to death, the family that can afford it makes a pilgrimage to Varanasi, on the holy Ganges River. There they engage a Mahapatra to care for the corpse of their loved one and to abide with and perform the rituals and tasks needed for transformation. The Mahapatra follows a series of ancient rituals: for example, anointing the corpse; wrapping it in brightly colored, gold-threaded winding cloths; and, in the presence of loved ones who have come there as pilgrims, burning the body on a smoldering pyre. They then begin the minute rituals designed to cleanse and educate and cosset the spirit along its way out of the waiting place. During this time, the *Atman* (the Hindu Self) perches on the shoulder of the Mahapatra, who, among other experiences, endures a most extreme hunger.

The Mahapatra remain responsible for the spirit for the next ten days. At the beginning of this time a pot with a hole in its bottom is hung from a tree. This pot becomes the abode of the traveler in the Waiting Place. The pot is filled with water and the traveler drinks the water dripping from the hole in the bottom. On the tenth day, the pot is broken and the traveler resumes its journey onward. Only at the end of the ten days, when the pot has been smashed, has the dead person made the transition from being a spirit inside a body to a spirit free of a body. During the period when the spirit inhabits the pot, it apparently retains a physicality of some kind, for the Mahapatra are constantly debating the size of a newly deceased spirit: Some consider the dead person's spirit to be the size of a knuckle, some of a thumbnail, and some precisely eighteen inches in height.

The ritual of the pots ensures that the spirit will remain in the Waiting Place—with the Mahapatra—while the necessary transformations take place. However, for the living, the ritual has its own function, bringing order and pacing to the crisis of loss. In this way, the Waiting Place gives rest to the living as well as the dead—rest, reassurance, and the opportunity for fear to sink away.

Mourning rituals that bring order in times of potential emotional chaos are familiar in most cultures. Another example is found in Judaism, which dictates a period of seven days of strict mourning— the period of *shiva*—following the death of a family member. During this week, the spirit of the dead person hovers around the living as the Hindu spirit hovers around the Mahapatra. According to the Kabbalah, the most esoteric expression of Jewish lore and law, during those first seven days after death, the spirit travels back and forth from its grave trying gamely to reenter its former body: Neither staying nor fleeing, it waits. Only on the seventh day, when it observes the damage done to its body by maggots, does the spirit realize that, yes, indeed, it is dead—and moves on.[7]

During these same seven days, the mourners sit together on hard wooden benches, all mirrors in the house covered with cloths. Most interpret these behaviors as reminders to the living that vanity and comfort distract and have no place in a house of deep mourning, but the Kabbalah teaches that these details have important meaning for the dead spirit as well. With the mirrors covered, the spirit cannot be fooled into thinking itself alive. Seeing its loved ones rocking on hard benches, rather than on the familiar furniture of every day, brings home to the spirit that something terribly dramatic has happened— something permanent, inexorable, that cannot be changed.

On the other end of the spectrum from the Jewish tradition of sitting shiva, mourning rituals in Bali involve the living in a series of lively activities. Here the body is often interred for as long as it takes the family to accrue enough money for a truly grand cremation, and so both deceased and living patiently wait. Even for the burial, there is much to be done. The body must be properly washed and dressed, a grave must be dug and fenced in, a casket must be built, a little mirror placed over each of the deceased's eyes to ensure that he or she will be strong, attractive, and sharp-eyed in the next life. A flower is placed in each ear to make sure that the sounds next heard will be beautiful.

Once cremation becomes possible and the big day is set, another complex series of preparations takes place. At every reasonably large cremation, at least one animal-shaped sarcophagus, life-sized or even larger, will be in evidence. Depending on the caste and sex of the dead, this might be a bull, cow, lion, deer, or fish-elephant. But all such animals will be four-footed, to symbolize the four brothers or sisters who were born with the body and, if treated properly, accompanied it, guarding and helping the person through life.

Next, a cremation tower is built. This represents the Balinese universe, the world-turtle at its base surrounded by two dragon snakes. Eleven tiers to the tower represent the eleven levels of Heaven and Earth and the world mountain.

Until the cremation day, a lamp is kept lit to guide the wandering soul back to its home, and usually a life-sized doll is made from old Chinese coins tied through the center with white thread.

On the appointed day, all is burned. A special percussion orchestra plays, and specially dressed dancers imitate soldiers in battle, symbolically guarding the spirit from evil influences. The sarcophagi are carried with much uncontained energy to the cemetery. The melee is meant to confuse the spirit and make it lose its way so it cannot return to haunt the family. People ride in the tower, and sometimes they let two young chickens fly free to symbolize the soul flying away. The direction the fowl take indicates the auspiciousness of the occasion, so nowadays the chickens are often deliberately thrown in a "good" direction.[8]

In these examples—the Hindu's careful treatment of the water pots, the solemn week of sitting shiva in Judaism, and the string of interrelated events in the Balinese response to death—time spent in a Waiting Place allows an interim, when the dead and living are still close and can communicate, if not directly to each other, then symbolically, across the divide. Both focus on the transition and the enormous adjustment to be made: The deceased must relinquish the baggage of life, and the community must relinquish the person from its midst. This is the last opportunity for dead and living to share time and space and, in the dual purposes of their rituals, most systems show a harmony between the living and dead and an easing of the separation.

GHOSTS

Nevertheless, waiting patiently doesn't always work to reconcile us to our fate when we die. After all, even dead, even in this first stage of the journey, we're still pretty much human beings, and we don't always do as we must. We ignore and then fight reality and, when that's no longer possible, we deny it. No matter where we've grown up, from the Mato Grosso in Brazil to the plains of North America to the highrises of Manhattan . . . many of us do not go gently into that good night, to borrow famous words from poet Dylan Thomas. Perhaps in all the world only a minority actually do.

An Array of Ghosts

Though most cultures understand ghosts to be simply those spirits who return to the living for one reason or another, others go into the subject with more detail. The Tanka people of South China have a range of ghosts quite carefully delineated and distinguished:

- Ghosts of Hell. These are ghosts that have been treated badly and have no place in the afterworld to dwell.
- Water Ghosts. These ghosts are the spirits of drowned people—as soon as a person comes who might witness one, a water ghost disappears underwater.
- Hanged Ghosts. As you might guess, these are spirits of people who have been hanged.
- Young Ghosts. These are young souls, who died before coming of age. Even though they have died, when they do reach the age of adulthood, their parents perform a marriage ceremony for the young ghosts. Young ghosts are also known as Grievous Ghosts, because they died before coming of age.
- Pig Ghosts, Cow Ghosts, Chicken Ghosts, and Duck Ghosts. As seems logical, these are ghosts seen mostly by farmers.
- Returning Ghosts. Souls return to their homes two to three weeks after death—so, quite literally, all who die become returning ghosts. When souls return, the bereaved family and all its neighbors must be careful to close their doors at night, some placing a red paper outside their doors to keep the ghost from entering. If a living person does meet a returning ghost, he or she is liable to experience great misfortune. So it is, as we have seen, in cultures all around the world: the return of souls from the afterdeath goes against the natural order, and the living act to encourage the dead on their journey.

Nankai Social & Economic Quarterly (1937, AF17 South China, 849–50).

In other words, the dead often fight the inevitable. Even after their prescribed time in transition, half in and half out of the body and within the ephemeral cloak of ghosthood, many will not leave. They refuse to move on.

The results are one of many categories of beings we call ghosts.

Ghost sightings are voluminously reported in the parapsychological literature, and much statistical research has been carried out on the general phenomena.

"In our surveys [Gallup], a substantial number of people on every educational level believe that the afterlife will be populated. Other studies we've done can help us refine these figures and beliefs even further. For example, one American in nine (or 11 percent of the general population) believes in ghosts. And despite the larger number of believers in the United States than in other countries on most spiritual issues, as many as 20 percent of the British believe in ghosts, with 7 percent reporting they have actually seen a ghost!"[9]

Particularly after those first twelve or so days—and it is striking how many cultures have settled on this number, or approximately this number, as comprising the first stage of the afterdeath journey—some spirits just don't want to leave, don't know how to leave, or aren't ready to leave. They want to return to life. They hover around their graves or their families seeking ways to rejoin the living. Sometimes they simply aren't ready to part with their possessions or the other trappings of their lives. Some are just too worried—they can't leave yet: Their children aren't grown, their work isn't finished, the family future is in danger. Sometimes the problem involves the rituals of death and mourning themselves: The living have handled the arrangements surrounding the death badly. Under such slipshod conditions, a spirit simply cannot continue on the afterdeath journey.

A senior researcher for the Fon in Benin, Africa, explained the import of following the burial rules: "Failure to respect funeral ceremonies results in the wandering of souls and confusion on earth. The deceased cannot reach the afterdeath. Some rules are to be respected during burial: white color, position of the dead in the coffin slightly leaning on the left arm with the head turned toward the hand. Only infertile women are buried lying on the back. There is a whole ritual to conform with. At night, such troubled souls do disturb the rest of those still alive."

Examples of discontented ghosts abound all over the world. A typical one comes from Native American tradition. "The Blackfeet believe," writes Clark Wissler, "that, when people die, their spirits do not start at once for the other world. They feel lonely and are unwilling to leave home and friends. They wander near their old haunts for about two months, when they seem to grow accustomed to the new conditions, and then start for the spirit world. Some are never contented there."[10]

In Nembe, West Africa, I met a mother and daughter who were plagued by nightmares, migraines, and other discomforts after the death of their husband and father. The women had become desperate and complained at length about the terrible tortures of sleep deprivation owing to the ranting and haranguing of their dead family member. If one couldn't sleep one couldn't live. Something had to be done.

So the women engaged a shaman, who confirmed their suspicions that the dead man was indeed still hovering nearby and was sending them the curses of headaches and insomnia. The man had died in the midst of a long family disagreement and had left his wife and daughter angry and distraught. The women explained to me as best they could: They had been careless, they supposed, with the funeral arrangements. They had been angry. He had treated them badly. Yes, all right. They had been hasty and impatient about the burial. And cheap.

So the man's spirit could not rest peacefully; nor could he or would he move on. He hovered close to the family, worried and worrying them as best he could with unfinished business. In short, a discontented ghost.

This shaman was a young woman with a beautiful round face and round eyes. She wore a gorgeous green and gold turban of African cotton and a matching dress that we would call a muumuu. This was an intense individual: I never saw her smile as she sat on her bench, legs apart, her skirt looped gracefully between her knees, and addressed the mother, daughter, and ghost.

As immaculate and colorful as was her outfit, her place of business was a little on the shabby side, disorderly to my Western eyes, with bottles, spears, bits of wood, and rags strewn in what appeared to be random fashion. The negotiation that ensued was marvelously pragmatic, not unlike other business transactions I have witnessed. First the widow talked, then the daughter; then the shaman expressed the ghost's point of view. Breaks were taken; water was sipped. At the end of four hours, a settlement was reached. The women would sacrifice three cows and four bottles of spirits in the name of the father. The ghost was exasperated; he had wanted *six* bottles. But somehow—to his consternation—he had admitted to shoddy behavior of his own toward the women just before he died. Reluctantly, he accepted the offer. Over the next week or so, the transaction was successfully concluded and the agreed upon sacrifices made by the shaman. The ghost quit his nasty ways, left the women in peace, and was able to depart and take up residence in the afterdeath.

THE PAIN OF COMMUNICATING

The pollster Gallup has determined that well over half of mourners in the United States speak to their deceased loved ones.[11] Most such visits occur soon after the death; their frequency diminishes as time passes. People describe these visits in a range of ways—from sheer, invisible, silent "presences" to detailed dreams and visions. Some of the visitors have no visible form at all. Some speak; others simply gaze silently. Some convey explicit messages despite their silences; some, just a feeling—of reassurance, or love, or sorrow.

From the day my father died, he and I kept in constant touch. It was our secret, and we had long, long talks: I didn't see him, but I felt his presence, and his voice was as clear and articulate as it had been in life. We checked in with each other constantly, and I thought of him as part angel, part ghost.

One day, I was participating in a meeting. Bored to tears, I called to my father and began chatting with him, just as I used to and just as I would have phoned up a friend out of the sheer need for diversion. But this time he spoke to me with a decisiveness that he hadn't used in our chats before: "I'm going now, Sara," he told me, formally calling me by my given name as the group chatter went on around me. "I can see you're happy. You have your work, your marriage. I'm going now, dear. Good-bye." And we never spoke again. From that time on I have never felt his presence or even the urge to contact him. Now that he has been dead for more than half my life, I am connected to him only by photographs and memories.

Years after our last encounter, in the course of my studies, I learned that I had unknowingly been very unkind to my father after his death. If you talk with people in touch with the spirits of the dead, those whose thought and work constitute the body of knowledge known in part as the occult, you will learn soon enough that visiting the living, and particularly communicating with living beings, can be excruciating for ghosts. They should be long gone from the Waiting Place and onto the next stage of the journey.

To learn more about the experience of ghosts and to keep abreast of developments on the whole spectrum of thinking on death and dying, in the late nineties I traveled to Mainz, Germany, to interview Ernest Senecowsky, a major researcher and great enthusiast in the field known as Instrumented Communication. This field of study concerns itself with what I call the engineers' afterdeath: It is a system filled with machines and wavelengths and calculations both on this side of death and the afterdeath side. To allow for contact with the spirits of the dead, the instrumented communicators switch a television on to a blank channel and turn a video camera onto the screen. In a scientifically controlled environment, to assure that they are not receiving data or waves from around them, they make and then play the video film backward frame by frame to find images there—sometimes a single image, sometimes a series of images with audio—of people who have died. Additional data from the world beyond death comes by fax and telephone.

My visit, during which I looked at fuzzy video images and listened to audio tapes, was like time spent on the set of a science fiction movie made in 1952. In his early sixties, Senecowski's English was good enough to allow him to proclaim frequently and with force, "Here is what is!" One of his most fervent points, which he confirmed with audio tapes and the work of a growing field of researchers in Germany, Switzerland, and America, was that for the dead, materializing and communicating with the living from the other side were absolutely exhausting—horribly effortful and, in the end, a magnificent contribution on their part. I could sense what he meant from the sound of the voices he played me: These souls made a strained, rasping sound like people who have had tracheotomies and have to go through the enormous effort of forcing air from their stomachs through their throats in order to vocalize their words.

Strange as the Instrumented Communications appeared, and as far out as their thinking may be, Senecowsky's correspondents made it clear that for the dead reaching back to the living involved extreme effort and pain. Spirits seem to *need* to move on, and the living can help them do so. This help might consist of, for instance, determining what precisely is keeping them from continuing on—unfinished business, perhaps, or insecurity about the fate of living loved ones, or overattachment to the habits and trappings of life as we witnessed in Nembe—and doing what we can to resolve these impediments. In short, if we care about our ghosts, we will not only let them go, but we'll help them go.

The Guarani Indians, a small group living on the coast of Brazil near the Atlantic Forest, have an extreme but not uncommon view of this need to encourage the dead, of whom they are terrified, into the afterdeath. When a community member dies, the living change their own names, burn down their own houses, pack up, and leave the area—hoping to make it impossible for a reluctant spirit to tarry, follow, and bother them. In writing about another group, the Fox Indians of North America, Denise and John Carmody describe a less radical approach, with a focus on the living:

> The leader of the clan would speak to the deceased, telling him or her not to envy those still alive. Rather, the deceased ought to press on, to the land of the ancestors in the west. After death there was a journey, and the first obligation of the deceased was to see it through. . . . By picturing the activity of the deceased as a movement

away from the village, the clan suggested that new obligations demanded a firm break. Psychologically, it seems clear that the clan was projecting onto the dead person its own need to make a clean break. However dear the deceased had been and however healthy it might be to treasure fond memories, life had to continue. It would serve no useful function for members of the clan to regret the death of any member too long or too passionately.[12]

Accustomed as we are to thinking of native cultures as far, far different from those familiar to us in the Judeo-Christian traditions, this description could be applied almost whole cloth to the mourning rituals of Judaism: "Do not unduly weep for a dead person, nor mourn him beyond measure. How long [shall mourning last]? Three days for weeping, seven days for lamentation, thirty days for bleached garments and for [the prohibition of the] cutting of the hair," explains the Torah.[13] Then the living must return to life (though mourning for a parent lasts a year)—the living must resume life and the dead one enter *Olam haba,* the world to come, a place not focused upon or described in the Judaic literature: ". . . of the world to come it is said: No eye has seen it but Thine."[14]

All around the world, the dictum is the same: If we love our dead, at the very least we must let them go and encourage them on their journey. How comforting it can be for mourners to have a task, a job to do in the face of traumatic loss. The concept of a Waiting Place, where the spirit waits and rests, can ease a transition that might otherwise appear abrupt, meaningless, and even cruel in the fear it induces.

Maxine's Analogy

For Joanne, whom I described in chapter 2, it was the idea of reunion that brought light comfort.

For Maxine, it was the idea of divorce.

"When my doctors told me there was no more they could do for me, I had the most familiar feeling—a kind of anxiety that was worse than the disease, worse than anything. I recognized this awful feeling but couldn't place it. Then I *got* it. It was the same way I felt when Gordon left me all those years ago. As if I were balancing on the edge of a cliff just about to go over."

After Gordon divorced her, though Maxine was a tenured professor with a million interests, she couldn't imagine life without him. They had had no children, and when she contemplated her future, she saw a shadowy nothing. The emptiness frightened her terribly, and she entered therapy.

Eight years later she returned, this time after receiving a terminal diagnosis of metastatic breast cancer. "Do you see? I'm facing the same thing again."

"Facing what?" I asked.

"Nothingness. Emptiness. An amorphous darkness."

"Are you scared?"

"Terrified. I feel this utter terror at the nothingness of it all. Just as I did after my divorce, when the old life was completely gone and I couldn't imagine a new one."

I reflected on Maxine's comparison. I asked her whether she could imagine a change in herself now similar to the one she had experienced after her divorce, the death of her marriage. Eight years ago, in that period of insecurity, Maxine had had moments of wavering—most people do after a divorce, experiencing profoundly painful and hopeless moments of doubt, longings to return to the safety of the marriage and to the familiar routine of everyday life, even at its most unsatisfactory. Like a ghost hovering above the gravesite of her marriage, she was already irrevocably in a new phase of her life but still found herself circling, in her mind at least, and longing to return to the site of the old.

Slowly, though, her vision had cleared. She had begun to see some ways to visualize her future after divorce, and eventually she had been able to leave the past behind. I proposed to her that there might be an analogous clearing of vision in a Waiting Place after death. In facing death, wasn't it possible that a "place" or "time" existed in which realities would be revealed that neither she nor anyone else had sensed except through art, the vital imagination, or visionary meditation?

"That's a deeply comforting thought," she responded.

Her longing to sense something, someplace, a meaning in the process of "disappearing," led Maxine to begin to draw. She asked her family to bring to the hospice facility her colored pencils and fine paper, and showing a surge of energy that surprised everybody, started drawing. Maxine, who had minored in art while she studied classics long ago, began by making simplified copies of Tibetan Buddhist mandalas, to which she had always been deeply attracted, visual embodiments of the process of meditation. This was her seemingly instinctive attempt to conceive of the inconceivable within a recognizable form. Never attracted to abstract art either as artist or viewer, she soon began adding detail to these visionary circles—creatures, vegetation, landscapes, and so on. At one point, I told her about Paul Beard's conception of Summerland, and with enthusiasm she incorporated the concept into her drawings, in many of them attempting to cast into image and color the things, places, and people—long dead or forgotten—that would bring her rest and comfort.

"Are you actually visualizing the afterdeath?" I asked her. "Yes and no," she answered, seeming not terribly interested in the question. "Well, yes, I guess so. I begin that way, but it's the act of drawing that quells my fear. When I'm making these circles and thinking so hard about what to sketch, they are all that exist for me. Yes, I guess in a kind of vague way I'm imagining something I might come to see. But it's the imagining I crave, not an accurate vision of where I might be going.

"I'll tell you what really helps," she told me. "When the drawing is really working I'm completely unaware of anything else, even my body, even to some degree the pain. It's just me melded with the drawing. I don't think I've had that wonderful feeling of complete engagement since I was a child. I feel as if I'm floating, my body no longer here."

Jonathan

Jonathan, one of the earliest people to be diagnosed with AIDS, gained no relief from visualizing the afterdeath as a journey. He was a well-known fashion designer who had been raised in the Midwest and found himself with no real community of support in those early days of the disease. In fact, he was pretty much alone in his endless struggle with opportunistic infections—and also with the social consequences of the infection: whom to tell, when, why, who could be trusted with the truth. In short, Jonathan suffered horribly both physically and psychologically in the early years of his illness.

In one session with Jonathan, I decided to broach a new subject. I had just read that morning of the Muslim afterdeath, a lush resting place just over the border from the world of the living where the good recline on soft couches to eat grapes and indulge their senses. Jonathan was a Christian; he prayed every night and was also a great indulger of the sensual. I thought the description of the anteroom to the Muslim heaven—this one for those who had lived the good life; the hell was hideous—might spark in Jonathan something to look forward to. I launched into a detailed description of what I had read.

Suddenly Jonathan was in tears. "No more, Sukie!" he cried. "No more! I can't take it!" Sobbing, these were the only words he was able to get out.

I stopped talking.

"I pray there is nothing," he managed to say after a while. "I pray there is just sweet nothing. I'm too worn out for anything else."

Suddenly I saw that Jonathan couldn't take the possibility of the very *more* proposed in the remainder of this book. Jonathan was sated with existence, in any form. Any more surprises, of whatever quality—even the lushest, even the grapes, even the solely imaginary—would push him past his limits of endurance. When I backed up and told Jonathan of the Waiting Place where he did nothing if that was what he wished, saw nothing if that was what he wished, thought nothing if that was what he wanted, his terror of the "more" ceased and he returned to the image again and again as a source of hope and comfort.

REFLECTIONS ON STAGE I: WAITING

Waiting is familiar to us all. Perhaps irritating to some of us, perhaps restful and refreshing to others, waiting makes islands of time throughout our lives. We wait for the right mate, then for the wedding, for the baby to be born. We wait for the degree to be earned and the promotion to be achieved. So we, the living, have Waiting Places too, on this side of death. However, instead of gaining from them, "lying fallow," as the English analyst Masud Kahan called it,[15] we are often impatient, feeling that the flow of our lives has been interrupted.

Life is filled with changes and small deaths—minideaths, I like to call them. We have all watched the demise of a marriage, of youthful ideas, of carefully planned careers. We have experienced the loss of our physical capacities, endurance, youthful appearance, important friendships, groups we've cared about. After each of these events there is the potential for us to enter into a Waiting Place. In reality, loss, no matter its nature, involves a time of mourning and simply waiting. Loss can also be a transition, just as in the Waiting Place where transformation occurs.

As a psychotherapist, I approach transitions with great respect, aware that they frequently hold the seeds of psychological growth. Transitions—our responses to the life changes that alter our reality—are never easy; nobody glides through them. Each one can be an event of tremendous personal meaning.

For both the deceased and the living, the Waiting Place is where the reality of change begins to sink in. Both after death and after a minideath in life, waiting allows us to rest. Time can soothe, even in the deepest crisis. In waiting, both the living and the dead find their direction slowly.

Roberto Assagioli, founder of the school of psychology known as Psychosynthesis and a contemporary of both Freud and Jung, spoke of bifocal vision—the ability to simultaneously hold on to or allow two realities, not just one, to exist in our emotional lives.[16] This capacity allows us to know despair while at the same time perceiving a tiny window of hope opening onto an unnoticed path. Such can be our experience in the Waiting Places of life and the afterdeath, when we perceive first darkness, then light *and* darkness—and then undreamed of possibilities that are slowly revealed to be real.

CHAPTER 4

Stage II: Judgment

A Moment of Judgment . . . Imagined

It is a formidable hall. The ceilings tower, and the walls are made of silky, shining planks of golden wood. The light throughout is bright, though it suffuses the magnificent chamber evenly. He has positioned himself before a panel of beautiful inlaid materials—woods perhaps or earth-toned stones. The pattern is mandala-like, drawing his attention to its center like the iris of an unmoving eye.

He has not been directed here or placed just so in the hall. Nevertheless, he has known just what to do—and knows with no doubt that he will experience his moment of truth here.

There is no delay, for there is no time here, and though no sound, sight, or movement occurs in the great hall, he knows the process has begun. Someone, something, is scrutinizing him. Something is reviewing and weighing his life, and as that process goes on, evaluation unwinds within himself as well. His history is illuminated, but not simply as memory. Rather, his actions, thoughts, goals, intentions, secret motives, and desires are revealed to him as factors in a mathematical puzzle. Its solution will become his destiny.

Nothing moves, nothing changes. Suspense afflicted him before the process began, but now he waits calmly to learn his fate. When he leaves the hall he will begin the next phase of his journey, his destination as inevitable, unchangeable as a village at the end of a road.

It doesn't take a religious scholar to understand that, despite the refreshing and welcoming idea of the Waiting Place, all in the after-death is not sweetness and light. In fact, one might even be a four- or five-year-old Christian child; a young Hindu of as few years, maybe fewer; or a Tibetan child of three to understand that once you've had your rest across the border, there's work to be done.

When the traveler has emerged from the chrysalis of physicality, it leaves its Waiting Place and enters the next stage of its journey, where its fate will be determined. What route will the traveler take? What will be the destination? What will be the result of the life just left—pain or pleasure, punishment or reward? In many systems, though by no means all, the answers to these questions are determined by a process all too familiar to us in the realm of the living: An implied deity, a representative of one, or even somehow the system itself scrutinizes, evaluates, and judges the spirit according to the life just ended and its destiny in the afterdeath irrevocably, inarguably determined.

Of the many aspects of the afterdeath landscape, judgment is the hardest to face. Many people turn to the ideas of "New Age Lite" for reassurance that no corner of existence is too hard and no personal responsibility too heavy. However, if you begin to explore the hidden corners of existence, you can expect to bump into the serious issue of judgment and its consequences. And judgment brings discomfort—self-doubt, suspense, fear of punishment. . . . A caveat: This chapter may make you squirm. At the same time, the ideas here may well seem familiar. Unlike issues of waiting, heaven and hell, or rebirth and reunion, this issue—judgment—is the ether of our lives. Each of us is a judge: Sometimes working overtime, we go about with our eyes darting here and there. Sometimes our personal sense of justice is so carefully calibrated that few of the actions and presumed motives of our families, neighbors, politicians, celebrities, and *by far* ourselves escape being weighed. Our assessing can even form a major part of the silent basis of our relationships. The notion of judgment in the afterdeath is a source of little comfort for many who contemplate the course of the journey.

Doreen

Doreen, a patient of mine, responded to news of her impending death with great agitation. In essence, she got on the phone and didn't get off until she was no longer able to talk. Rather than attempting to "get her affairs in order" in the conventional sense, Doreen became obsessed with calling everyone and anyone she had ever known since childhood. Her point was to apologize for whatever harm she might have done to anyone in her life, inadvertently or otherwise.

There was a frantic feeling surrounding these calls. It wasn't that Doreen felt she had been such a bad person, but she knew she had given a million unintended slights and unrecognized insults, just as most people have without even noticing. And the certainty of these incidents gave her nightmares: She was obsessed by the question of what would happen to her after she died, when she came up for judgment.

"In my dreams I'm all alone and having to answer for myself to an invisible judge," she told me. "And all the pain I've given, all the less-than-generous thoughts I've had about others, reenter my consciousness as I present myself. I'm just miserable and terrified."

The joy she had given, the love and generosity with which she raised her children—none of this counted to Doreen. She focused solely on the pain and the, to her, unendurable possibility that she'd be judged a bad person and consigned to eternity in hell.

She phoned and phoned until she died. Many of those she tracked down hardly remembered her, let alone the "sins" she had committed against them. But Doreen persisted, and it made sense that she did. For she had always been a self-scrutinizer and self-judge to the most minute degree. Sad as it was, it came as no surprise that a terminal diagnosis would cause her to focus with fear and distress on the judgment phase of the afterdeath journey and do all she could ahead of time to acquit herself in order to try to come out "clean."

Doreen was not unusual in focusing her fears on the scrutiny she would receive after death. Many of us know people who, on the brink of death, have suddenly shown remorse for the lives they've lived. One of the most dramatic and explicit examples of our own day has emerged from the political arena, where cruelty, ridicule, and the effort to ruin an opponent have become prominent. How poignant it was to see Lee Atwater, chairman of the Republican National Committee under President Bush and well known for his particularly uninhibited attacks on the public figures who raised obstacles to his president's political goals, step forward with public apologies and regrets after receiving a terminal diagnosis of a brain tumor. Was it fear of leaving a tarnished image behind that motivated his regrets— or was it the terror of judgment *after* death that suddenly loomed before him, casting a new light on the ways of the world he had subscribed to so wholeheartedly?

Most people care deeply about how they will be remembered and, like Doreen, in facing death frequently become acutely concerned with returning to old relationships to acquit themselves with grace. But the potential imminence of judgment *after* death can be equally, if not more, unsettling to a person concerned with having lived a good life and reaping just rewards. No more weighty and meaningful turning point exists in any of the afterdeath systems I have studied than Stage II, when the spirit is scrutinized and judged for the way it was lived—though frequently it is unclear *who* or *what* is exactly doing the scrutinizing and judging. Two ultimate questions arise at this point on the journey, questions to be answered inexorably and irrevocably:

- not only, "Am I bound for rewards, pleasures, blessings, or punishment, condemnation, isolation, and sacrifice?"
- but also, "What was the meaning and purpose of the life I am about to leave? Have I caused pain to myself and others? Have I lived a life with nothing but empty achievements? Have my efforts amounted to something positive that will reap for me positive consequences? In short, have I lived a life that contributes to the larger reality in a positive way?"

THE METHODS OF JUDGMENT

As with the notion of Waiting Places, it is only the more "goal-oriented" afterdeath systems of the world that set a spirit at a crossroads and determine its fate based on its past life. Other afterdeath methods allow a smooth, natural slide from one world to another, perhaps with a bit of friendly collaboration between living and dead.

Two art works come to mind that highlight the contrast between judgment-oriented and nonjudgmental systems. One, "Lord of Six Conditions of Rebirth" (held by the Musee Qumet, Paris Museum), is a Buddhist scene of Divine Judgment that is a dazzling web of color, figure, and image: Multiple bridges span a pool, connecting upper and lower regions. Above the pool is the Paradise of the Supreme Buddha, populated by an array of radiant beings fascinating to the eye. Below, seated on a throne, is the Bodhisattva Ksitigarbha, a Buddhist deity whose job it is to intercede with the Judges of Hell. Around the Bodhisattva float six figures on scarves representing the "Six Conditions of Rebirth." The painting is a sea of motion and complex symbolism reflecting the complexity and significance of judgment in the Buddhist afterdeath.

Compare the description of the "Lord of Six Conditions of Rebirth" with that of a beautiful Eskimo stone-cut stencil drawing titled "The Dying Man Becomes a Wolf" (held by the Winnipeg Art Gallery). Here, an Eskimo girl eases her father's passage into the other world by singing a magic song with magic breath. With her help he will enter the body of a wolf and eternally hunt the caribou in the Beyond. The father passes through to another world and eventually, with no accounting and no crossroads on the path, is gone.

In the systems that do rest on judgment, four distinct types emerge, some with known judges, some without. I've given these four types titles that reflect their basic methodology and that distinguish them from one another. These four methods of judgment have been found to exist in most afterdeath systems, and although some systems of the afterdeath entail no judgment at all and others use more than one method, when we leave the Waiting Place most probably we will face judgment, whether it be by the Tallying, Karmic, Evolutionary, and/or Challenge Method.

The Tallying Method

The Tallying Method is analogous to the balancing of a checkbook: quantifiable units of good—good works, good thoughts, good behavior, good beliefs (the money earned)—are added up and weighed against quantifiable sins (the checks written). If a spirit comes out in the black—in some forms of Christianity this means if one's actions and behaviors reflect one's belief in Christ as the Son of God—then the goal, eventual reunion with God in Heaven, is guaranteed. If the balance comes out in the red—a quantifiable sum of sins unbalanced by belief, good works, etc.—one is adjudged to Hell.

The ancient Egyptians had an afterdeath judgment method of the tallying kind. There, the spirit used magical formulas—some learned in life, some written as reminders on a tomb or pyramid—to move from one stage of the journey to another. Finally one reached the site of the judgment of the soul's worth, the Hall of Double Right and Truth, there to address a committee of forty-two god-judges. The soul confessed its sins: "I have done injury, spoken lies, robbed with violence, and caused pain."[1] Then the heart, to the Egyptians the seat of the consciousness and symbolic of the soul, was measured against a feather. If the scale remained balanced, the soul proceeded to the pleasures of paradise. If not, the tally was inarguable: The soul went on to Hell.

The Egyptian Way

In the coffin is a false door to allow the deceased to move. Also there is a painted table of offerings to provide sustenance; a plan and description of the Field of Hetep, which is a version of paradise; and a list of ship's parts, information useful to the deceased, who joins the sun god in his bark and guides it through the sky.

Another plan, or map, is painted on the inside surface of the bottom of most coffins: of a blue waterway surrounded by mounds to represent the day sky, and a black land route, surrounded by water, representing the night sky. This plan, along with text from a document known as *The Book of the Two Ways,* is meant to identify certain uncommon demons and some commonly known terms for places in the afterlife. This book is really two different books—one a geographic guide through the landscape of the afterdeath and another detailing certain spells. If the deceased knows the spells to the first stage, he will become a star in the sky with the moon god, Thoth. If he knows them to the next stage, he will join Osiris in his mansion. And if he knows all the spells he will join Re on his bark in the sky.

Adapted from Mircea Eliade, Ed., *The Encyclopedia of Religion*, vol. 5 (New York: Macmillan, 1987), p. 41.

At one time, though Judaism has no afterdeath as such and concentrates on life rather than what follows it, in the folklore of orthodox Jews two angels accompanied each person through life. One, at the person's right shoulder, recorded the good deeds; one at the left recorded the sins. When the time for judgment arose after death, a third angel, a "sunlike being," stepped forward to take the two records in its hands in order to weigh the righteous deeds against the sinful deeds. "On the day of the great judgment every *measure* and every *weight* and every *scale* will be exposed as in the market; and each one will recognize his *measure,* and according to his measure, each shall receive his reward" [italics mine].[2] As in the market, one's destiny becomes a matter of balancing the checkbook.

This pair of Jewish angels has much in common with the beings reported by one of our Hindu senior researchers. "Things are beyond your control in the next world," said this participant in our study, a Mahapatra who cared for the dead on the banks of the Ganges. "What you will do and what will happen to you are factors decided by your actions in this world. As long as you live on earth, there are two *shravanas* [supernatural beings], one on each shoulder, who, every night while you sleep, go to Yamaloka and give an account of your actions throughout that day to Chirragupra, the keeper of the 'account books,' who makes the appropriate entries. This becomes the basis of what you will receive; pleasure or pain."

It is in the Christian tradition, and particularly through its richly evolved universe of art, that the rewards and punishments resulting from the Tally Method gain the form and substance that give them so much weight, even today. We have centuries' worth of paintings of heaven and hell, but no painting approaches the detail attained by the finest of Christian poets: Dante Alighieri, chronicler of the Christian afterdeath.

The method of executing punishments—most graphic, tortuous, and often ironic punishments as described by Dante—shows the Tally Method of judgment at its simplest. If a spirit is found to be "in the red," Minos, a shaggy, furious man/beast, functions with relish, carrying out the decision of the judge. Minos the gatekeeper is a monstrosity with a terrible tail. Slowly, his tail approaches the sinner to wind itself around its body: The tail chokes the air out of the penitent. To which circle is the poor spirit destined? The number of times the tail circles is the level of hell to which the spirit is sent. Having completed his calculations and curled around and around, Minos raises his tail and hurls the spirit below for all eternity.

In the Tally Method, once the judgment has been made, there are no arguments, no questions, no explanations. The judgment is quick, to the point, and icily quantifiable. Still, as a clerical friend of Victorian novelist Anthony Trollope is reported to have said, "Without a certainty of hell's eventual punishment of the successful but wicked, life on earth would be unbearable."[3] The terrible mathematics of the Tally Method speaks to this human need for justice done at last.

Interestingly, eternity doesn't always claim the sinner forever. As with an overdraft at the bank, under certain circumstances there are ways to work things out. In Dante's description of Purgatory, unlike his vision of Hell, souls execute the patient work of expiation. Here there is more light, more hope, than in Hell, and eventually one can climb up from the "foul air" of Hell through nine levels of Purgatory toward Heaven. When that happens, all souls in Purgatory rejoice and sing hymns at the release of the redeemed soul.

The Karmic Method

If you live in California, you hear that word *karma* a lot. "Wow! You must have amazing real estate karma!" "Gee, what did you do in another life to give you such terrible health karma?" Perhaps the principle is captured to some simplistic degree in these light-hearted throwaways, but the complexity and subtlety of this system as expressed most fully in the Hindu and Buddhist religions are not even hinted at. If the Tally Method of judgment is a simple checkbook or calculator model, the Karmic Method is a computer manipulating a near-infinity of interrelated details. How many thoughts, actions, intentions make up a life? The answer is inestimable. If you consider the interrelationships among the myriad variables, then you begin— only begin—to sense the complex web that determines the Karmic Method of judgment.

The Karmic Method determines the sum total of all these possibilities of human endeavor and their ethical consequences, resulting in a single judgment of the nature of the next life to come. Will we return to life in reduced circumstances—as a camel, perhaps, or a dog—as a punishment for our karma? Or will our judgment bring reward, in the form of a more elevated life than the one we just left—the life of a well-respected scholar or teacher, perhaps even a governor? Most desirable of all, might we possibly attain the ultimate and sweetest of all goals: that of slipping off the tiresome, demanding, energy-draining Wheel of Life into one of the levels of Nirvana, a state of ineffable peace that is *beyond* all heavens, free from the world of space and time? Nirvana is a state of liberation, spiritual freedom, true health, and immersion in—integration with—the cosmic consciousness.

One hot day in the holy Indian city of Varanasi, where Hindu pilgrims bring their dead to enter the afterdeath, Edmundo and I sat leaning against a wall with a Mahapatra interviewee in the shadow of a dusty building on the banks of the Ganges. Around us swirled the ceaseless bustle of life—and most particularly life devoted to the care of the dead, as corpses and their parties passed us by on the way to the burning grounds. Amidst this cacophony of life and death, I asked our companion to explain karma.

"Oh, but, my! Karma is the root of *everything*," he said, appearing to wonder how to begin. "Let me tell you a story." He stretched out his long skinny legs.

"A man died from snakebite," said the Mahapatra, "and the Snake was brought to court and asked why it had bit the man. 'Death told me to do it,' answered the Snake. So Death was called onto the docket. 'Why did you tell the Snake to bite the man?' 'Time told me to,' Death answered. And Time was called: 'The man's Karma signaled me to come,' answered Time. Karma then answered, 'It was the man's Soul that called to Death.' But the Soul inside the man reported that it was the man's Mind and Intelligence that had forced the Soul to call. Mind and Intelligence pleaded that there was something the man had eaten that had led them to speak. But Food blamed Livelihood—if the man had worked at something else, said Food, he would never have eaten what he had.

"The moral of this story? Ah. The meaning of the tale?" he asked, grinning. "The moral is that one should not support oneself by unacceptable earnings that will lead one to eat corrupt food, for corrupted food corrupts the mind, which in turn upsets the soul, and so on down the line. There's nothing random and unconnected, and nothing in a person's life that does not have an effect on the next. And you see, this is a short version of the story—it could go on so much longer. Each and every thing is connected to the others, each changes the others, each puts a new understanding on things. To have a good next life, one must be very, very careful all the time."

How careful we must be is suggested by the fact that the highly sensitive method of judgment that is karma lies even outside the power of the gods to affect. Consider another Hindu tale:

One day, as the gods were lazing about, a young upstart god challenged the idea of karma, calling it cruel and its irrevocable judgments too unforgiving.

"Oh, karma is far beyond our control," responded the elder gods.

"But you are gods!" said the youngster. "Surely you could intervene."

"Let us show you what we mean. Watch," cried the gods. They peered down to earth and saw a beggar trudging along a wooded path. He carried all his worldly goods in a sack upon his back and was bent and broken by life. "Now, watch!" cried the gods, and into the beggar's path the gods above hurled a very big but light sack filled with gold. But the beggar paid it no mind, stepped around it, and trudged on.

"Keep watching!" cried the gods and took up the sack to hurl it again, this time hitting the beggar on the back. The beggar continued on, unaware.

The story goes on and on, with the gods placing the sack first between the beggar's feet, then on his head, then under the tree where he stops to rest. But always, always, the beggar remains oblivious, living out his karma, the destiny determined by the past deeds of his life.

The Tally Method of judgment brings with it the conviction that in life people can alter their destinies by earning more credit. And, theoretically at least, such gains inspire joy in fellow travelers—witness the hymns and hallelujahs rising up from Dante's Purgatory when a sinner earns escape. The overwhelming complexity of the Karmic Method, however, brings with it a kind of fatalistic neutrality—we can *try* to earn progression into a finer life next time, but a neutral acceptance of our fate in the face of the immutable universal computer may be the more appropriate response to judgment.

The Evolutionary Method

In what I call the Evolutionary Method, the universe is seen as consistently evolving, and our lives are judged with respect to how we contribute to this evolution of the whole. With this method, each of us has a dual purpose in both life and death: to evolve as an individual and to add in some way to the universe.

This grand idea—of the individual in collaboration with the forces of a greater reality—takes many forms. It is the driving force behind the religion of Baha'i, which focuses on spiritual progress not only as the goal of human life but as the source of human happiness, both before and after death. For followers of Baha'i, judgment, such as it is, results from the soul's own inner commitment to take the steps needed for a spiritual evolution toward God. In this context, reward and punishment are tightly linked to this single goal: Those who systematically strive and move closer to God experience the joy of fulfillment; those who fall away from the spiritual goal bring the judgment of a lack of joy.

A more occult expression of the evolutionary model is found in Theosophy, a worldwide movement developed in the 1800s by the controversial visionary Madame Blavatsky. In this spiritual tradition, the spirit is also eternal, here climbing the ladder of being through a series of rebirths until it reaches the status of perfect being. Ascending spirits are helped in this progress by those called Masters, who have gone before.

Both in Baha'i and Theosophy, there are no outside judges. Rather, the judge is oneself. Specifically what the spirit of the deceased person evaluates—having reached, rested, and been transformed in Summerland, for example—are not so much their actions as the *intentions* behind their actions and the consistency with which the intentions coincide with the direction of the evolution of a universal consciousness. Here, in the Evolutionary Method, there are no whippings, no strangulating tails, no angels standing close by weighing every thought and action. Instead, the spirit itself reflects on the life it has just led as if watching it unroll on a screen—but the watching is not a mere set of observations by which to judge. We *experience* the effects we had upon others of our every thought and action.

This self-evaluation following death can be excruciating. We experience not only the memory but all the hurt we have caused; feel our heartbreak at our own selfishness; perceive with no rationalization our indifference to others; and see, acknowledge, and boldly feel through empathy the terror and chaos we may have created for others as we moved along through life. In this process, we relive our lives in palpable indentification and empathy with those we have harmed. We face our deepest intentions—our hidden motivations and secret reasons for the way we behaved. Masters or great teachers make these intentions visible, and we see them revealed as if watching a huge movie screen. So, we might see ourselves practicing compassion—while making quite sure that others notice that we are compassionate. We might see ourselves raising our children to be happy—but only for the purpose of raising proud reflections of ourselves, the "ideal" parents.

The Evolutionary Method may seem benign at first, a kinder, less objective method of evaluating than straight tallying or the computing of karma. But it is a fierce judgment method, demanding that the spirits of the dead look at themselves with unprotected eyes. As a result, we look at ourselves afresh as naked souls, stained and bruised with the results of our selfish intentions and motivations that we know to be so deeply human.

However, despite the experience in the afterdeath of seeing our lives for the first time without defenses or blinders, in Baha'i there is joy in eventually finding one's way into the evolutionary stream toward God. And in Theosophy, after stripping ourselves and facing the truth, we find ourselves in the First Heaven, where, having done our painful work of confronting the evil within us, we become free to live as souls in beauty and love. In the lovely First Heaven, Beard gives a particularly detailed depiction of the afterdeath that resembles a utopian university full of noble architecture and blessed by the mildest of climates—our spirits again begin to evolve. There, among much else, we learn to enter and reenter the dimension of time so as to communicate with those on earth, sending telepathic messages to the living through dreams. On earth, those still alive experience these communications from deceased loved ones as wise resolutions, deep insights, and a sense of guardianship that, in turn, urge loved ones toward the path of pure intentions.

In the First Heaven, the first stepping stone after Summerland, mentoring the living is an opportunity for spirits to expiate the soiled and spoiled intentions they have identified in their period of painful self-scrutiny. In this way, spirits' judgments of themselves gradually lose their painful negative qualities to become positive contributions to the totality of the universal evolution.

The Challenge Method

Tibetan Buddhism's system of judgment is unique in the world, both in scale and grandeur. All other methods pale before the rich, evocative imagery of the afterdeath in Tibetan Buddhism and the gauntlet of scrutiny a spirit must run there. I call this the Challenge Method of judgment because it consists of a series of events that seem brilliantly designed to make the spirit lose its way. Failure in this method can mean rebirth in a lowly form, and only a string of successes in the face of increasingly terrifying challenges reward the spirit with the ultimate goal: escape from the Wheel of Life to a place in one of the many heavenly states called Nirvana.

In the evolutionary afterdeath system of Tibetan Buddhism, the spirit operates either karmically or evolutionally (see box). It begins to face the series of challenges four days after death, the Waiting Period determined by the Tibetan system for the soul to detach from the body. Although ultimate judgment is indeed affected by the life just left as well as by the state of mind at the moment of death, the more potent determinant of the traveler's destiny is how it will navigate the upcoming challenges. The series consists of forty-nine events, staged in what I have been calling the afterdeath but what by Tibetan Buddhists is termed the Bardo state, an intermediate state between lives.

The Judge of Death, Dharmaraja

In one Tibetan Buddhist conception of the moment of judgment, Dharmaraja presides over dead souls filing through his hellish palace. As befits a decider of destiny, Dharmaraja is huge and red and holds a sword in his right hand and "the mirror of justice" in his left. Before him, as he sits on his throne and rests his feet upon a lotus, are geniuses—white and black and all born simultaneously—who shake from sacks white and black stones, representing deeds from the lives of those to be judged, into separate piles. Completing the scenario is an animal-headed scribe, who will record the judgment as the souls file through.

As the people to be tried step up, the stones are weighed against an iron weight. Those judged to have lived bad lives are sent to various hellish tortures: from places of glowing fires to those of freezing cold to woods of threatening sword-leaf trees. But a beautiful path leads away from the scene for those who have attained release: Along that path they proceed toward a paradise to the west.

The challenge itself consists of ancient images that Buddhist teachers and scholars understand as manifestations of our own all-too-human psyches. In other words, strange and terrifying as it is, the imagery of the challenges comes from within us. Evoked rather than created, these detailed forms are representations of our own greed, lust, ignorance, desire, pride, envy, and hatred. Paraded before us in this way, their horribleness is now visual, menacing, and distracting. Here is a taste of some of the challenges as described in rich detail in *The Tibetan Book of the Dead,* translated and with commentary by Francesca Fremantle and Chogyam Trungpa:

- The fifth challenge occurs on a day that is green, and the quality of the vision has the ephemeral nature of air or wind. Amoghasiddi—a manifestation of Buddha in one of his many forms—appears, in this particular image associated with action, fulfillment, and efficiency. Nothing can stand in its way; it is unstoppably destructive energy, associated with the realm of the jealous gods. A spirit encountering Amoghasiddi would be hard-pressed not to retreat, intimidated and confused.[4]

- The green light of the animal world, symbolizing ignorance, permeates the seventh event. Five Herukas with three heads and six arms each appear, representing the outrageous, exuberant quality of energy that cannot be challenged. And a second type of wrathful energy appears—dancing on a corpse to extinguish thought . . .[5]

- The eighth event is a meeting with a wrathful, blood-drinking deity dark brown in color with three heads, six hands, and four feet firmly postured; the right face is white, the left red, the central dark-brown; the body emits flames of radiance; the nine eyes are widely open, in [a] terrifying gaze; the eyebrows quiver like lightning; the protruding teeth glisten and set over one another. The monster gives vent to sonorous utterances of "a-la-la" and "ha-ha," and piercing whistling sounds. The hair of a reddish yellow color, stands on end and emits radiance, and the heads are adorned with dried human skulls, and the symbols of the sun and the moon. Black serpents with human heads form a garland for the body. . . ."[6]

As these examples show, the detail, color, and vitality of the Tibetan Buddhists' afterdeath are nearly overwhelming. Each of the forty-nine dramatic, colorful, and most energetically staged encounters is a test and a challenge of the traveler under scrutiny. What is the correct response to the appearance of monster after monster, each one more pointedly threatening than the one before? What must the spirit do to be adjudged successful in negotiating each increasingly disconcerting event? The answer is found in these five lines from *The Tibetan Book of the Dead,* quoted by Sogyal Rinpoche in *The Tibetan Book of Living and Dying:*

Now when the Bardo of dying dawns on me
I will abandon all grasping, yearning, and attachment,
Enter undistracted into clear awareness of the teaching
And eject my consciousness into the space of the unborn Rigpa
[pristine awareness].
I will know it to be a transitory illusion.[7]

"I will know it to be a transitory illusion." Simple but difficult. In response to the forty-nine events arising in the Bardo state, if the traveler reaches out, hesitates, cries, screams, dodges, or shrinks in fear—despite the intensely personal nature of the event, if the traveler believes even fleetingly in the reality of the threatening monster—the test is failed and harsh judgment is passed. Personal as each encounter may be, engaging as it may be, dramatic and exciting and terrifying as it may be—all is illusion. There is no other truth.

"I will know it to be a transitory illusion" tells us not only *what* to perceive in the name of truth—that all is illusory—but also *how* to perceive it: by remaining undistracted. In essence, the forty-nine events are nothing *but* distractions from the fundamental truth of illusion. To perceive steadily the truth that all is illusion, no matter what passes before us, we eminently distractible human beings must practice, practice, practice remaining focused on the truth and immune to diversions.

How is this possible? Through "serious and sustained reflection"—in a word, meditation.

Meditation is of the essence of Buddhist practice in life, but its value extends into the afterdeath as well. Meditation is the means by which the traveler prepares for the forty-nine encounters in the Bardo state in order to acquit itself with calm understanding. This unique continuity of purpose across the boundary of death is reflected in the practice of reading *The Tibetan Book of the Dead* to both the dying and, during the forty-nine days following death, the deceased.

The point of reading from *The Tibetan Book of the Dead* is to remind travelers that all is illusion, to anchor them against distraction, and to provide them with a low and steady chanting voice to facilitate meditation. Of all the instances of collaboration between living and dead, this is one of the most intense, and perhaps one of the most beneficial for both traveler and living person. As the reader reads on, reminding the traveler of the nature of reality, which is illusion, so too does the text reinforce the reader's own understanding of illusion and the value of "serious and sustained reflection."

WAYS TO JUDGMENT

In many systems and cultures, the spirit's journey toward its fate is acutely suspenseful and can be horrible—as horrible for the damned as it is blessed for those headed for paradise. Lovely to me are the images that symbolize the movement after the moment of truth: Very often in the literature of the afterdeath they are bridges or ladders.

Bridges have deep symbolic value in many living systems. In Jungian dreamwork they can be tools of transformation, and in Greek mythology bridges allow for the spanning of difficulties, spiritual and emotional as well as physical. In afterdeath systems bridges are often a means of shuttling spirits along—and can be not only the transition but in and of themselves the determination of what our destination might be.

The Sulawesi of Indonesia have a complex system of bridges on a long and difficult afterdeath journey—"but a strong buffalo," a senior researcher told us, "will help you through." Their dead must cross the Salu Bombo, or the Souls River. Five spans cross the river, each one for a different class of souls: There is a gold bridge for the aristocrats and a palm-tree leaf bridge for the slaves and spirits who met unnatural deaths by spears.

The Bridge of the Separator

In a Zoroastrian Judgment of the Dead, the deceased cross the Bridge of the Separator. To the wicked, the bridge is sharply angled and edged, nearly impossible to navigate. Haunted by memories of the evil actions of their lives as they attempt to cross the bridge, they inevitably lose their balance and fall into the abyss of Hell.

When the righteous pass over the Bridge of the Separator, though, this same span is smooth and comfortable, completely accommodating. They pass over the bridge without any difficulty at all and slip easily into Heaven.

Islam has the Sirat Bridge, which stretches over Hell and leads to Heaven. This bridge is thinner than a hair and sharper than a sword. In the Islam religion, judgment—determined in the Tallying Method by the weighing of the Books of Deeds—takes place all at once midway between Heaven and Hell, on the bridge itself, which was first crossed by the great prophet Muhammad. It is as if the bridge itself judges. The righteous spirits simply walk across Sirat Bridge with ease, but the sinful have to crawl across, dragging their guilt. Inevitably, the latter fall into the flames of hell leaping below the bridge.[8]

Sirat Bridge is remarkably similar to the Chinvat Bridge of the Zoroastrian religion. Zoroastrianism was the ancient religion of Iran, the first of the world's "institutional" religions to introduce the concept of judgment and the idea that life on earth had consequences in the afterdeath. Here too the bridge is the centerpiece of judgment, and many descriptions of Chinvat Bridge are found in the Zoroastrian literature. In suspense, the spirit makes its way to its afterdeath destination:

There is a sharp edge which stands like a sword, and Hell is below the Bridge. Then the soul is carried to where stands the sharp edge. Then, if it [the soul] be righteous, the sharp edge presents its broad side. . . . If the soul be wicked, the sharp end continues to stand edgewise, and does not give passage. . . .⁹

Perhaps even the most sinful spirit can fool itself with its first step onto Chinvat Bridge, but by midspan the spirit's fate is decided, and the consequences of its whole life determines its destiny.

Ladders, too, represent pathways to destiny in the afterdeath—one goes up to paradise or down to the dark depths. In an account of the funeral of an Ijo priest in southern Nigeria, an observer describes a ladder as actually participating in making the judgment on the fate of the dead priest's spirit. "Turn your hand," those holding the ladder are instructed by those officiating at the funeral. In response, the ladder turns in circles, and the direction those circles take proves the dead person innocent or guilty of sorcery, which in turn has an impact on his destiny in the afterdeath.¹⁰

JUDGMENT: IMMERSION IN THE TRUTH

My client Doreen died in high anxiety, as she had lived all her life. She had always been a fierce self-scrutinizer and overly harsh judge of her own behavior and had worried about going to hell since she was a little girl. Up through the final days of her life, she was still thinking of people to call, apologies to make, old sins and indiscretions to smooth over.

I had little success in helping Doreen break through her self-blame and diminishing her anxiety. But I thought how she might have shifted her perspective slightly in order to contemplate the final judgment that had her so frightened.

The answer I came to is inherent in all the methods described above: the balm of truth.

In each method described, judgment is scrutiny, evaluation, and the decisive crossroads between punishment and reward. But looking to the *context* in which judgment in the afterdeath invariably takes place, we find an environment of pure, unadulterated, liberating truth. Truth in the afterdeath is so unlike that which passes for truth in our lives that the closest comparison I can come up with is between the clearest snowmelt stream and the water of a polluted lake.

When my colleague Edmundo Barbosa is not accompanying me on interviewing expeditions around the world, he is practicing psychotherapy in his specialty, helping groups and individuals cope with terminal diseases. In his work, he has a special relationship with the truth: He seeks it, attempting to liberate his patients with its healing power.

"I tell stories—stories of other people, stories from literature, stories and koans and small examples from the world's religious and spiritual traditions. Something of the Tibetans. Something of the Cree Indians. Something of my neighbor down the street or a client I knew ten years ago, what he feared and what happened to him. These might seem like false constructions, nothing to do with truth. But the story goes into the mind, and the person goes home and thinks of it over the week, passes the story on maybe to a wife or a husband or a child. And very often the story itself breaks through the resistance to an acceptance of death.

"For the stories *aren't* false constructions: They are carriers of the truth. Telling them is a way to slip the truth inside the brain, where they can—not always, but can—work against the denial of truth and suddenly bring down the walls.

"What I have seen is this: Accepting the truth that you are dying enables you to achieve a state I heard described in Nigeria by this deeply evocative phrase: 'This man is ripe to die.' Ripe to die. To me, this phrase contains a sense of natural progression, and in the progression of nature is basic truth.

"Let me put it this way. Think of a tree, a living system. A fruit on that tree is part of the system, and when the fruit is ripe it's at its fullest—flavor, taste, nutritional value: it is ripe to feed. And therefore it is ready to leave the system of the living tree to serve the life around it. In my practice, a client who is ripe to die no longer resists but accepts the truth of his or her dying. Inevitably, then, that person takes practical action to 'feed' living loved ones with the fruits of his or her life—writes the will, pays the taxes, ties up the business, works out problems in the family. But more than that are the benefits to the dying person of stepping fully into the truth:

"Strife ends when truth prevails; one need no longer struggle. To resist truth is pain; to accept it is to enter seamlessly into reality. Many people suppress the knowledge of impending death out of fear of dying in the here-and-now and fear of harsh judgment and punishment after death. But with truth comes the knowledge that the pain is in the resistance, not in the truth. And along with the struggle, fear can disappear as well.

"The second benefit is riskier to explain, for there is as far as I know no scientific confirmation of it. But my long experience with the dying has convinced me that denial increases the agony of death and, conversely, acceptance—readiness, or ripeness, and embracing the truth—brings ease.

"One boy in a cancer group gave his voice to the significance of this possibility. 'When I came here,' he told us in the group, 'my greatest fear was how I would actually die. Everything I had ever heard told me that there was great pain and suffering connected with dying of my disease. I was terribly afraid of pain, but I was equally worried about my family seeing me in agony. And what I'm finding here, as people in this group die week by week, is that—well, one week we are here and the next week we're gone. So death can come much simpler, much easier than I thought. And to me that changes everything, and I am not afraid.' "

Esalen

"And the truth will set you free"—it's certainly not a novel insight but it is an important one. An illustration comes from my days as a group leader at Esalen Institute, a world-famous personal growth center on the California coast. Eventually most people there spend a certain amount of time together in the wonderful Esalen baths, hot natural springs overlooking the ocean. Exposed to the view of all is an indescribable array of bodies—fat, smooth, thin bodies; wrinkled and sagging bodies; beautiful bodies; bodies that show the wear and tear of long and bumpy lives; highly imperfect bodies; augmented bodies;

bodies with scars, mastectomies, missing testicles, fat stomachs, colostomies, and other surgical changes. Almost everyone strips down and first enters the baths with awful trepidations, fearful of humiliation and completely convinced of their secret ugliness.

In five-day workshops we used to run, we would do an exercise to address the power of truth. We would ask participants to point out both the best and worst of their own bodies, to "show us the part of your body you are the most ashamed of and the part you are most proud of." Invariably, as we went around the circle, group members would point out the best part first. "I love my muscles, my chest hair, my breasts," they would say. Or "I've bicycled for years and have very slim thighs." Or "I like the way my arms look when I hold them horizontally." And then came the hard part: pointing out the "worst parts": the scars, deformities, bloat, veins, bony protrusions, and fat.

Most people were profoundly moved by this exercise: to be confronted with so much private, human truth, rarely expressed. Sometimes, though, a group member—in the spirit of truth telling—would say, "You know, I hate to say it, but that mastectomy really *is* sort of strange looking," or "What *happened* to you?" The result would be a very tense stretch of suspenseful silence and then—and this was most frequent—a cry combined of laughter and tears from the person under scrutiny. The cry would be an expression of relief. Finally, he or she would explain, after years of dressing in closets, the dreaded words had been spoken. This participant had entered the baths with the horrible anticipation of repelling the others, the explanation went, had been worried about it all week, and had thought hard and long about not showing up at all. And the worst had indeed happened: The truth had been told. What he or she had suspected others might think had been proven the case. Inevitably, after that first round of laughter and tears from not only the particular member but from among the group, someone would speak to the relief of sitting with the truth: the wonder that nobody had actually died once the unseeable had been seen and the unsayable had finally been voiced.

Judgments in those magical baths, in those magical groups, could be as affirming as they were negative. It was not uncommon to hear, "So that's a mastectomy? I always thought it would look really disgusting, but you know, it's really okay." Or "Look at the swoop of that scar! It's really quite beautiful!" Truth: It has its surprises, but above all, both in life and death, truth can be a source of relief.

AFTERDEATH SYSTEMS WITH NO JUDGMENT

Over the course of our lives, all of us have been judged and all have passed judgment on others. Both sides of the judgment experience can range from painful to downright excruciating. To judge is isolating and distancing from others. And to *be* judged is isolating and distancing from others. Perhaps all our lives we have craved understanding; now, in the afterdeath, some of us rankle under the fulfillment of our wish. But in some systems, there is no judgment at all.

For many Mexican Indian groups, the only difference between life and the afterdeath is the skeletal form we take. And the Yoruba Hunters of Nigeria see the afterdeath as identical to the lived life; after death one steps into the landscape and takes on a familiar existence. Learning of these and others like them helped my client Eleanor.

Eleanor

Eleanor, a thirty-six-year-old advertising executive and a client of mine with cancer, believed with all her heart that she had caused her own disease. This was a belief I had heard expressed far too often from both colleagues and clients. The torture that this egocentric credo added to the problems and pain of cancer never failed to elicit my anger, and whenever a patient expressed this point of view—an attempt to claim complete control and responsibility for a complex and devastating diagnosis and disease—I had to struggle to remain calm.

To Eleanor I responded with a fake awe—which she did not notice—saying, "My God! How *did* you accomplish that?"

People who consider themselves responsible for their terminal disease assume themselves to have great personal power, even if that power is ultimately vanquished. Eleanor, cut from this cloth, responded with all sincerity, "Oh, it was the stress. I couldn't control my stress! I let it run rampant in my life, in my family. I never stopped to meditate, to concentrate on my breathing, to do all the stress-reduction techniques I've known about forever. I just *indulged* myself, I guess, never taking care as it built up. The cancer was the result. I brought it on myself."

Articulate and well learned as her response was, I wasn't buying it. "What you say doesn't make sense to me, Eleanor," I said, abandoning all pretenses. "I know many people who don't meditate, who never concentrate on their breathing, who are stressed out beyond belief, and who don't have cancer."

But Eleanor repeated her rehearsed text. "If I could only relax, let go, breathe, go with the flow, take each hour as it comes to me without fighting it or being scared or worried," she cried, "I'd be healthy. But I'm just not strong enough to do it. Something in me won't relax."

Her self-judgments were overwhelming, and my anger got the best of me. "How in hell can you possibly relax with a diagnosis of rapidly spreading cancer?" I demanded, my voice rising. "This is crazy thinking, Eleanor. How you live your life *with* the cancer, what you do to *affect* it now that it's here—over that I believe you can have great control. But to believe that you have caused the cancer itself is nonsense and actually pretty arrogant on your part. No one claims to know how cancer starts. Cats get cancer. Trees get cancer. Do you believe that they cause their own disease, too? I have never seen a stressed-out tree, have you?"

No answer this time. My words reverberated in the room. We sat in silence.

And then this harsh judge and jury rolled into one asked a question, "Are you sure cats and trees get cancer?"

"Yes," I responded. "It's not the same cancer we get. And we can't get it from them. But it *is* cancer and it *is* as devastating. The cat and the tree die from it."

Eleanor had no response. Our first hour together was over. As I said good-bye, I wondered if she would return. I wondered if I had been too harsh, if I had misjudged her inherent strength, and if my visceral anger had been too much in the lead.

But Eleanor did return, and for the next month we repeated and repeated this first session, albeit with some variations. In essence, Eleanor would judge herself from a godlike point of view, I would debunk her judgments, and the sessions would end in silence.

Slowly we began to talk about judgments—both how important they were to her career in a positive way, and how tortured she had been by them as a fat, acne-plagued, overweight adolescent. When were judgments helpful? we wondered together. And when were they not?

As Eleanor's illness continued to devastate her body and bring her closer to death, she expressed a fear of how she would be judged after she died.

"No one could be harsher than you," I replied and we laughed. But the question was an important one, so I told her of visiting Nembe, a small Nigerian village.

As Edmundo and I realized in our time there together, learning of afterdeath systems that do not judge the dead at all can come as a soothing surprise to those who assume from childhood that they must account for themselves, both in life and in death. David, the Oxford-educated grown son of our senior researcher, took us on a stroll in his father's tiny hometown of about three hundred people, pointing out the houses of friends and family, grandparents, uncles, and boyhood playmates. He waved and called out politely, and we waved, too, and from some houses people called back. In others, silence reigned.

Suddenly Edmundo asked our host, "David, are all these houses inhabited?"

David laughed. "Well, in one way or another," he said. "We bury our dead here either in their houses or in a new house built just for them. In this way they stay with the community after they die. Trouble is, though, we're running out of room, and some people are trying to convince the village to build houses on the outskirts of the town the way you have your cemeteries. But so far it's not a popular idea— nobody wants to miss out on anything after death except one man.

He's a hermit who hates to talk and keeps to himself. He's the only one willing to have his house after death built outside of town."

Whatever they were, whatever they did, the Nembe dead remained a part of the community. Here in Nembe there was no elaborate method of accounting, assessing, and deciding. The nonjudgmental afterdeath system preserved the community and kept its population intact. Death in Nembe was a mere technicality.

The story struck a chord with Eleanor, she later told me as had my remarks on trees and cats. She marveled aloud at the possibility that the afterdeath might be judgment-free. I brought in the pictures Edmundo had taken of Nembe, of David our guide, and of the houses of the dead and living. Eleanor asked to keep one. I had it framed and gave it to her as a gift when she went to hospice care.

REFLECTIONS ON THE JUDGMENT STAGE

One of our great clichés is the beautiful deathbed scene free of judgments and filled with love and gentle grieving. But those of us left behind, as well as the dying themselves, don't necessarily fit this picture. We are often wracked with guilt and made miserable with harsh judgments of ourselves and the dying. How can we forgive ourselves for trying to figure out how we'll exact payment for debt from the executor, remembering—being unable to forget—the mean-mouthed sarcasm in which the dying person recently indulged . . . wishing that the dead person had died sooner. "How *could* I? I'm so ashamed" is a commonly heard lament.

Some of us judge ourselves guilty for doing too little. "My sister deserved more than I could give." "My father shouldn't have had to go through that, and yet I did nothing."

Some of us judge the dying; we want them to die the "right" way: "Why isn't he meditating?" "Why isn't she filled with the love and light that is come?" "Why doesn't she fight more?" "Why isn't he making amends?" and the worst, "Why did she *choose* to die now?"

As human beings, we tend to be self-referential. Slowly, from infancy, when we experience ourselves as the sun and our parents the
planets revolving around us, our vision of reality widens, but flashes
of our centrality remain. So it happens that we judge ourselves, sometimes very harshly, for developments in our lives, and we judge the
dying in much the same way.

We can't stop the process of our loved ones dying, hold it back until
certain matters have been taken care of or until *we* are prepared for
their deaths. We must be careful not to impose on the dying our
myriad judgments of how they should die, just as we must be careful
not to impose on ourselves our myriad judgments of how we should
act as witnesses. If the majority of the afterdeath systems of the world
hold true, when we die, judgment awaits us all. We need not waste
precious time at the deathbed and afterward in evaluation and blame.

As we pass through the Judgment Stage we reach a closure. With
final judgment, the spirit is liberated from uncertainty, ambiguity, and
the suspense of waiting. The spirit's intentions and behaviors are
reviewed by one method or another, its future is determined, and the
traveler is propelled forward on its journey.

CHAPTER 5

✑

Stage III: Possibilities

A Heavenly Realm . . . Imagined

Sparkling, the crystal foliage of the tree taps lightly in the breeze. She is arrested by the gentle sound and stops to sit beside the trunk and watch the blue-white light of the realm break up through the transparent leaves. Nearby a stranger projects his enjoyment of her pleasure in the tree. This projection is itself a small visible geometric shape, bubble-like in its delicacy and only as long-lived as it needs to be to convey its meaning before it dissolves in the soft air.

She is grateful for the thought and sends back a shape of her own, one that carries her appreciation of the humor and sharp interest of the stranger. Also present is a question: What stream of thought do you work on?

The other composes an answer, and the result, when it comes, is surprisingly complex: I am a student of balance, it tells her, and its many impediments.

Balance. The concept as it is expressed in the softly whirling bubble construction is a difficult one to interpret. She is not sure she has it right, and a query swims out from her almost involuntarily.

Balance, the other sends out once more, among the numberless aspects of the universe; among past, present, and future; among nearness and distance; among inner and outer—the infinitude of being. If our balance is too rigid, we overwhelm the force of interconnection; if it is too tentative we dare not enter in. You see why the calibration of this quality takes careful, minute study.

Back and forth float the beautiful molecule-like constructions as the crystal leaf music plays lightly in the breeze. She takes in his answers as

*she would take in water: They enter her own thought stream, nudging
and tipping and pushing along the small stones—ideas—that line the
channel.*

Varanasi is a holy site for Hindu and non-Hindu pilgrims alike. Even
the most irreligious of visitors can experience satisfactions of spirit
made visible in the rituals and customs—many associated with
death—that are performed there in the open air, often on the wide
steps, called *ghats,* leading down to the holy Ganges River.

But Varanasi is also a hot, teeming city—noisy, full of dust, and
overflowing with demanding hordes of children with a sharp eye out
for tourists. Edmundo and I traveled there to research the
Mahapatra—keepers of the rituals of the dead—and went straight to
the Ganges. We wanted to experience everything we could about this
place of pilgrimage and death, so we headed to the river in dual roles:
objective data gatherers and tourists.

The tourist role came with a mandate: One *had* to take a sunrise
boat ride past the *ghats,* where pilgrims from all parts of India took
their morning ablutions in the holy (and unspeakably contaminated)
river water. Beautiful as the people bathing appeared in the orange
sunlight of dawn, exotic beyond words though the cows were in the
smoke of the crematoria, ghastly and crude and unbelievably striking
as the scene appeared to one who treasured her private bath perhaps
above all personal rituals, at five in the morning, gliding along the
Ganges in a narrow, rickety boat, I craved my coffee like a drug addict.
Edmundo, too, exuded irritability—this over breaking his camera.
We were cranky, sullenly annoyed. The boat trip completed, we
trudged heavily up the *ghat* one behind the other and tried to find our
way through the crowds of pilgrims and hawkers back to a thorough-
fare where we could catch a taxi to our hotel.

We hadn't progressed far when suddenly we were passed by a line of
men running in the opposite direction, toward the river, chanting
rhythmically and carrying a wrapped body on a simple stretcher high
on their shoulders. We stepped aside on the path to let them pass. A
few more steps and another party ran past, chanting lightly with a
corpse as their burden—quickly followed by another. We gave up

climbing toward the warren of shops where the city began and stood by the side of the path we had chosen to watch the corpses being carried by. Unknowingly, we had stumbled upon a route to the preparation grounds. Body after body passed us, carried by bare-chested, barefooted men. Rhythmically they chanted, *Ram naam satya hai:* "Only God's name is true." The chant, signaling the mortality of the body, is very hypnotic, especially as accented with the pounding of bare feet.

Suddenly, a gust of hot wind blew up, and dust and ashes swirled around us, debris from the funeral pyres burning close and far along the river. As the ashes fell upon us, everything—of the city, of the crabby morning, of our personal, touristy, human concerns—dropped away. Small grumpinesses and emotional and bodily needs all blew away with the hot breeze, which coated our clothing, our hair, our eyelashes with dust. Like statues, we stood silent and transfixed, unaware of how much time had passed. Nothing mattered during that time of condensed nature. We were surrounded by and literally tasting of the palpable intermingling of life and death. No longer a concept, a starting point, a symbol or metaphor, death was in our eyes, coating our lips, and making our hands sticky in the heat.

Naked *being* was gently raining down on us as dust. Not only the fleshy world that most of us, most of the time, consider the chief reality but also dead bodies, and presumably hovering spirits, swirled around us in a mix of perceptions as we stood motionless alongside the path. Spirit animated our own bodies and those of the thousands of pilgrims and children and merchants along the *ghats,* but not the bodies held high overhead by the lightly running men. The spirits had gone—but where? I stood within the swirl of life and death and wondered.

Edmundo and I and our colleagues had been collecting data on "someplace elses" for several years now, traveling the world and asking questions, returning home and collating material. I had seen many dead people in my life. But not until I stood on that dusty path with the chants pounding in my ears and the thumping footsteps reverberating through my shoes did the journey away from the body—in all its implications and mysteries—become wholly real to me. That day Edmundo and I shared that rare and grand experience of total engagement, facilitated by the vital imagination.

THE VITAL IMAGINATION ... REVISITED

You will remember that the vital imagination gains us access to hidden realities. Profoundly deep and open, this function of our perceiving mind allows us those moments of hyper-reality in which the imagery of what we see combines with our deepest emotions and sharpest insights to create a coherent reality rich with meaning. Perceptually, the detail of these experiences is as sharp and memorable as we are capable of apprehending. Emotionally, the deep feeling evoked is utterly consistent with those filigreed perceptions. And *intellectually*—perhaps I should say metaphysically or existentially— the meaning inherent in those emotion-infused perceptions are profoundly satisfying to the searching human spirit. These moments of perception through the vital imagination are milestones in people's spiritual lives, and those who have them never forget them.

So it was for me—and for Edmundo, as it turned out—that day on the Ganges. Perhaps in response to the sight of the corpses or the chants of the carriers, patience, will, profound awareness, and a kind of faith that there was meaning here combined to plunge us deeply into the heart of the moment. The odd thing was that I experienced and remember this deeply meaningful stretch of time as a still point, one of the quietest of my life. Here was a riverscape teeming with life—merchants, animals, little children shouting for attention, and the stench of blood, fecal matter, urine, and polluted water everywhere. Hot sun, flies, fleas, ravaged dogs: There was no end of disruptive, demanding stimuli all around. And yet the deep feeling and meaning carried us out of that ragged, sensate level onto another perceptual plane.

What I saw there was wondrous: sunlight dancing off the rocks, a rhythmic movement shared by the living people, a sense of music investing the pallbearers, and gold woven into the cloth catching the rising light. All the smaller flecks of light seemed part of the greater illuminations, which were the funeral pyres that took the gold-threaded fabric wrapping the bodies and fed the flames with them. I could hear the whoosh of that special fabric and then feel the ashes that gently rolled down upon us.

That day on the Ganges—which had begun with so little promise—became the most precious of the trip. Just such moments, an infinity of such moments, are what yield the immense diversity of the afterdeath—the vast and, above all, *varied* collection of imagery shared by the world's people.

EXPECTATIONS AND POSSIBILITIES

For me, quite unexpectedly, the realm of death in a city of ashes was a place of meaning so deep that my experience there became a permanent touchstone, and my sense of certainty, of rightness about my work, deepened inestimably on that path. Without anticipating or expecting anything more from that day than a grueling string of obligations played out under the cruel Indian sun, I suddenly found myself on the other side of a barrier. On one side were common, everyday perceptions of a corner of a city devoted to death and dying: It was depressing, hard on the families who had brought their loved ones to die there, and more than a little ghoulish as a tourist attraction. On the other was a shimmering vision of the place of death in the order of nature, a vision that entered my consciousness permanently and from that day forward influenced my thinking about death and the afterdeath.

It's a cliché that expectations alter our perceptions. Expect a gloomy day and you miss seeing the rainbow. Conversely, expect to adore a famous poet and upon meeting him, you may never notice that he's really a colossal bore. More to the point, think about death and clench with fright, expecting only a painful passage into nothingness, where not only is all light extinguished but all identity as well. Or, rid yourself as best you can of all hackneyed images of death and beyond, and you are primed to consider the realm upon realm of possibilities that constitute unknown reality.

Barbara

My client Barbara, a passionate amateur artist, was fifty when she entered therapy, looking worn and tired. She had had cancer of the colon for three years, and the disease was steadily advancing. The pain was well contained and she had lived longer than expected. Her family—husband and two teenage sons—urged her into therapy, hoping she would find a safe haven there in which to discuss her fears of the future.

Barbara enjoyed our sessions, as she had hit upon something on her own that tapped in deeply to her resource of strength. While she was still hearty enough, she determined to write a memory book for her two sons to convey things about her life she wanted them to know. Of particular importance to her was describing the trip around the world she had taken as a young woman. This was one of the profound experiences of Barbara's life. The trouble was, she had taken the trip in 1968, just after completing her MFA degree in art school. This was 1992.

"And my memory is horrible, Sukie," she worried. "Menopause, cancer drugs, whatever—I can't remember what I had for breakfast. How am I going to remember Kenya twenty-four years ago?"

"Try," I urged her. "It's such a wonderful idea. Just try. See what you come up with."

What she came up with was . . . everything. She began with a detail: the eerie hot darkness she stepped into upon debarking from a plane in Khartoum in the middle of the night. And, like a string of beads, detail followed detail, memory followed memory: Smells, colors, sounds, people—and not generic people, but individuals— encounters, conversations, transactions in markets all over Africa, the Mideast, and the Far East. She remembered taking her first bite of French toast fried in ghee in a tiny Ugandan restaurant. She recalled a beautiful copper bracelet that an Iranian woman wore, and how the woman caught her staring and smiled over her veil. She remembered jacaranda and flame trees burning their colors into the dusky African twilight and the sounds of a train adding to the loneliness of a gray Turkish landscape. Barbara could hardly keep up on her computer with the amazing flow of details that had remained in her memory for a quarter of a century.

"The thing about that trip," she told me, "was that I was really an incredibly stupid traveler. I didn't read about the countries I passed through, I didn't know their history, didn't know their politics, didn't know the dangers some of them held for a wide-eyed young girl like me hitchhiking through the countryside. But I absorbed everything I saw. I remember wondering when I got home after traveling for a year, "How am I going to make sense of all my impressions? How am I ever going to sort through everything I saw?"

"But you did, didn't you?" I asked.

"Well, I did, to a certain degree." She was an imaginative woman with an expansive view of life. Occasionally she brought in drawings and paintings to show me, and I could see evidence of that long-ago journey: a series of Mideastern women chadors, myriad drawings of East African mothers and children with the beautiful textiles of their clothes highlighted. And now, in the memory book, Barbara was rendering the many realms she had passed through that year and reveling in the wealth of detail. Often, she would bring in a chapter and read it aloud in a session, and I would delight in her experiences and observations.

"There's something to be said for ignorance," I mused. "It can be dangerous and restrictive, but look how open you were to everything the world gave you that year. Experience, reality, possibilities just poured in!"

Writer George Leonard has used a phrase that perfectly captures Barbara's perceptual experience: "soft eyes." On that trip, she moved through the world with no resistance to her experiences—no expectations, no anticipations, and apparently even few interpretations. Soft eyes, soft ears, soft senses in general: The essence of Barbara's stance in the world was an openness to all possibilities.

Barbara had a way with words, and with simple directness she recorded her year of travel for her sons. When she died soon after completing her memory book, it became the most precious possession of the family.

THE JOURNEY RESUMES

An openness as free as possible of expectations combined with the inestimable diversity of reality—that appears to be the potent formula that keeps us open to new possibilities. Thus, we can respond to the fruits of the vital imagination—our own or others'—regarding the unseen realms of our universe. By contrast, the life of the resister of possibilities, the refuser of the presumption of *more,* seems down-right impoverished, anemic. All of us know people who have lost their openness, whose inner and outer lives are reduced to recapitulations of what has come before. Same job, same four walls, same diversions—and, at some point, all hopes or dreams faded, with none to replace them.

Openness to possibilities is the essence of Stage III of the afterdeath journey, maybe even its fuel. This openness stems from that moment of judgment in Stage II, when, by one method or other, the truth of the person's life determines the spirit's destiny. By virtue of the judgment passed upon it, the spirit moves through the myriad landscapes of the afterdeath on its way to a destination.

It is in Stage III, where the possible goals of the journey are revealed, that the world's cultures offer up the greatest array of possibilities. From a starry emptiness in the sky to a jeweled paradise a-flow with milk and honey, from a lonely path through a spooky forest to a baroque hell of perpetual tortures—the realms of the afterdeath to which spirits travel are nearly infinite in their topographies, inhabitants, and qualities. It is here, along the spectrum of possibilities, that the full potential of the vital imagination is expressed.

POSSIBLE REALMS OF THE AFTERDEATH

Here, then, is a cornucopia of afterdeath images, drawn from different parts of the world. The point is in no way to be comprehensive—it is not possible to present an encyclopedia of the afterdeath but rather to give a taste of the range of differences that exist and the power of possibilities that might well await us. It is exposure to the richness and contrasts among the many concepts of the afterdeath from around the world—the wide range of answers to the single question, "What happens to me after I die?"—that can free us to consider the possibilities and then believe as we choose.

So here, in Stage III of our journey, is a survey of the possible realms to which spirits go. These descriptions—though often passed down from one generation to another in an oral rather than written tradition—are frequently indistinguishable from art.

Simple Sketches

Some afterdeath geographies are nothing more than single, simple ideas. For example, here and there throughout the world many different peoples—Australian aborigines, Goajiro Indians, Inuit Eskimos—describe dead spirits as simply flying up to enter the Milky Way. Many Australian aborigine myths tell how the person's *birribir*—a deeply spiritual part of the soul—climbs up a possum-fur string (a particularly delightful detail, I think) to be transformed into a star in the Milky Way and merge with the power of the Sky Heroes."[1]

For the Goajiro Indians of South America, the Milky Way is the point of no return in the afterdeath journey, but even then "our soul is not lost," they say. "Only our bones are lost. Our bones and our skin. Our soul goes on its way, that's all."[2] The Inuits refer to the Milky Way simply as the road the dead must follow, and if you step out into a clear night in the country, away from the glow of the city that dims the stars, you will see the comforting presence of that road overhead—far away but glowing with the eternal presence of millions upon millions of souls of the dead. There they are, visible and present to the living every night. Remember these beliefs and the heavens will never look the same again.

The Familiarity of Home

Some accounts of Stage III of the afterdeath are idealized versions of life on earth. For example, many of those interviewed among the Yoruba of Nigeria (the source of the Candomble beliefs in Brazil) described a beautiful, brightly illuminated community that "is like earth in shape and form but is better than the world of humans." "In heaven—" a Christian missionary term absorbed into the Yoruba vocabulary—"in heaven, as on earth, people farm, hunt, and do business. . . . The environment is peaceful and the vegetation green and flowery. There is perfect peace—no thieves, no quarrels, no fighting, nothing to threaten the natural order of existence." This Yoruba saying captures the small difference between the worlds of life and death: "Earth is a market, heaven is home."

These are comforting ideas—the afterdeath seems homelike and familiar. For example, the Sulawesi of Indonesia make it very clear that "castes still exist in the afterdeath. Everybody is in his place and has to behave as he had in his place on earth." One Yoruban respondent told our senior researcher with notable confidence and calmness, "Dead friends are found in heaven in great number. When you die, you go and join your long dead early friends with whom you play. To prove this, we often meet deceased friends in dreams. Dead members of the family are in heaven, and when a person dies, one goes to heaven to join one's lineage, taking up the lineage, profession, and character that he had in life."

However, life on earth and the idealized life in the afterdeath are not always identical. "There are ethics in heaven above," says a Yoruban respondent. "Because of this, we often warn our recent dead, 'Do not eat millipedes, do not eat earthworms. Whatever they eat in heaven, you should eat with them.' This is a gentle warning, a way of saying that one should conform to the approved manners of heaven and not be a rebel against the established rules."

The Fon people of Benin, West Africa—the group that describes the web of living things that die and are born together—tell of a convenient means of learning the ways of the afterdeath. In their culture, beginning at ninety years of age, elderly people who have reached a high level of knowledge take part in two worlds: that of the living and that of the dead. These elderly mavens often deliver messages to the living from the spirits in the afterdeath, and they can tell people in the community about where they will go after they die.

Light

Light, a visible form of pure energy, is important in most spiritual systems of belief. In Jungian dreamwork, light can symbolize spirit. In the Christian tradition light stands for many things: grace, charity, belief. Christ himself is called the light of the world. Similarly, in Maori mythology—the Maori people of New Zealand—light is the primal father.

This spiritually rich and supportive symbol appears in the after-death systems of many cultures, too. In fact, afterdeaths throughout the world are suffused with a beautiful and often very unusual light. "In 'the beyond,' " says a Guarani Indian respondent from Brazil, "there is only clarity. It is always day and the sun always shines. Time goes by, time flows, and day never comes, nor does light. Eternal life is day. It is always day. It rains, there is rain, but the sun never goes away. The sun shines on life: eternal life."

John, the Christian author of the biblical Book of Revelation, makes a similar observation in his description of heaven, which he calls the Holy Jerusalem. He tells of a walled city of twelve gates made of pure gold, like clear glass, and decorated with precious stones. Then: "And the city had no need of the sun, neither of the moon to shine in it: for the glory of God did lighten it. . . ."[3]

When clients refer to the fearful, empty darkness of death, I mention these beautiful descriptions of unearthly light.

Trees

My client Mark had AIDS, and his diagnosis came early in the epidemic. At the time, an AIDS diagnosis was a death knell. There was no AZT, people were only beginning to admit that they had the disease, and there were few support groups. Mark's doctor told him to get his papers in order, that he probably had six months to live. The night after this terrible day, Mark had this dream: "I am walking. I come upon a tree. It is big, deeply rooted, reaching high to the sky. It has many branches and one leaf. The leaf is green."

"How do you feel about the tree?" I asked.

"It's beautiful," he responded.

"And the leaf?" I asked.

"Even more beautiful," he responded.

"But the tree only has *one* leaf," I said.

"It's enough," he said.

"Why is it enough?" I asked.

"Because it means that leaves are possible."

Among the many possibilities that the afterdeath can hold for us is a landscape containing special trees. Most often such trees are far more abundant than Mark's dream tree: beautiful, nourishing, and often supernatural in what they produce. These resplendent trees embody the themes of fertility, growth, change, and fruitfulness.

As noted before, Judaism as practiced today has little belief in life after death, but this was not always the case. Ancient Jewish literature describes an evolving topography. First there was She'ol, a dusty valley of bones where everyone went after death, regardless of the quality of their lives. Nothing grew in She'ol; the place was a dusty, bone-strewn desert. In more recent Jewish writings, though, an actual Heaven appears and, at its center, in one description, grows a tree of life, where God rests on His visits. The sweet odor of this tree is indescribable, and the tree itself is made of gold and crimson but is as transparent as fire. From the tree's roots flow four streams—honey, milk, oil, and wine—in four different directions.[4]

In an Aztec Paradise

In the Aztec paradise Tlalocan, the rain god Tlaloc sits at the base of a magnificent tree with health-giving rain pouring from his hands and awaits those who have died water-related deaths. On either side of Tlalocan, priests make offerings and plant seeds in the fertile earth. Below, souls play games, sing songs, and chase butterflies. In this glorious and most earthly of the three Aztec paradises, souls remain for four years before being reborn into another life.

Legend from Borial Image 214, "Souls in Tlalocan Play"
Artist Unknown

The Buddhists have their heavenly trees as well, some clustered together in a magical stand:

This paradise is full of magnificent vegetation, including trees that change their appearance six times a year during six different seasons. There are other trees that display the dazzling glory of all six seasons simultaneously, and some that show red and blue lotuses in full bloom. The majestic tree known as the celestial coral tree also grows here. Even musical instruments grow on trees in this paradise.[5]

In a Mayan conception of a paradise, a place of eternal pleasure, there is no pain or suffering, abundant good food and sweet drinks abound, and spirits find eternal rest under the branches of and shade of the *Ceiba* tree.

Though not a tree, a different sort of plant form is central to the afterdeath journey of the Ojibwa Indians of North America. In this account, the soul that has just died, "still fully conscious and still possessed of all human longings and desires," journeys to the land of the dead where it finds a giant strawberry—one single giant strawberry. If the soul takes a bite of the strawberry, it can never return to the land of the living. If a soul refuses a bite, it *might* manage to return—but only after it is suddenly seized from behind by the Skeleton-Woman of the Land of the Dead, who will break open its skull, scoop out its brains, and substitute a piece of moss for them. This is the Ojibwa way of completing the transformation from ghost to permanent spirit.[6]

Heavens and Hells/Time and Space

Within the cornucopia of possibilities are those systems that emphasize judgment, and the familiar concepts of Heaven and Hell emerge as concepts and images. The following description of Heaven comes from the Sufis, a mystical form of Islam. Heaven has golden walls with silver bricks (reminiscent of the apostle John's description of the Holy Jerusalem), the earth will be made of saffron, and all the inhabitants will have faces as radiant as the full moon. There will be no bodily functions such as urination, defecation, and so on, but spirits will eat and drink whatever they please, and will not grow old beyond the age of thirty-three, the age of Jesus. There will be four streams (as in the Jewish paradise, where streams flow out from the crystal tree) of wine, milk, honey, and water, and spirits will quench their thirst in abundance, a wonderful luxury for a desert-based people. And the wine, forbidden to Muslims in life, will be served by beautiful *houris*—voluptuous young girls—and handsome boys.

The Sufis promise beauty in abundance in Heaven—the *houris* wear fabulous clothes of delicate brocades and lovely silver jewelry. The sound of running water pervades paradise with a calming effect. Equally, in the Sufi vision, Hell is highly realized: Sinners will roast in a burning fire, drink water from a boiling spring, eat food fouled from a thorn plant. Once they roast they are given new skin so their torments can continue. In one tradition they are bitten by scorpions as large as mules and by serpents as big as camels. And the sinners themselves have huge tongues and continually vomit blood.[7]

One Buddhist version of Hell offers a contrasting, but equally horrible possibility:

First, the wardens of hell will drive red-hot iron stakes through the victim's hands, feet, and chest to prevent him from struggling. Then, using the sharp razors, they will shave off his flesh, head downwards. Next, they will tie a chariot to his trunk and force him to pull the chariot to and fro across a space blazing with fire. Then he will be forced to climb up and down a fiery mountain of red-hot embers. From here, he is taken into a huge boiler full of melted copper, where he is thoroughly boiled and hurled into the Great Hell, where he remains in flames for a long time.[8]

And suddenly, as in a movie building to a horrific conclusion, keeping us in suspense as images surpass each other in intensity and horribleness, the Buddhist spirit is released back into the known world. Life resumes and the memory of the terrible punishments recedes.

These descriptions of heavens and hells are really a form of shorthand. They use familiar symbols to sketch otherworldly, afterworldly, scenes. What they don't convey is something almost beyond our comprehension: the absence of time and space. Time and space as we understand them are measurement systems that are limited strictly to the world of the living. Perhaps the closest we can come to experiencing existence without these orderly constraints on reality are certain physical or mental "peak experiences," in which athletes, creative artists, and just regular people report that "time stood still," "the miles were as nothing," or "I was outside time and space."

Brazilians and Africans provide the words we need: They distinguish between *Aye* and *Orum*. "*Aye* is the physical dimension where all visible phenomena occur and all physical beings, including humans, exist. *Orum* is that immeasurable spiritual space—the Beyond—where the orisas and other spirits dwell in untouchable but ever present reality."[9]

Many believe it possible for the dead to break out of nontime and nonspace to rejoin and communicate with us. But no one ever implies that pushing through the membrane is easy. Instead it is suggested that the effort of reentry accounts for some of the difficulty of such communication.

Angels, Guides, Guardians, and Companions

In all the possibilities described worldwide, few human spirits are left to find their way alone through the afterdeath landscape. Some are, though: Sulawesans seem to seek their way to Soulland with only the aid of a good strong buffalo, and Fon spirits have little help in searching for their family areas in the "country of the dead." Aztec travelers who were poor or who died of disease—considered an unnatural death—had to try to reach their destinations in the afterdeath by themselves and faced awful obstacles on the way: mountains that threatened to move together to crush them, huge snakes with hideous maws, terrible crocodiles, eight deserts and eight mountains to be crossed, and then a peculiar challenge—a wind consisting of sharp flint knives.[10]

In most conceptions, though, guides or guardians and both comforting and challenging beings populate the afterdeath or cross travelers' paths at certain points along the journey. Particular kinds of characters recur—ferrymen, for example, who take spirits across rivers in the afterdeath landscape. Charon was the boatman in Greek mythology who ferried spirits across the river Styx. The Ijo of West Africa have ferrymen as guides, too: "They are responsible for ferrying people from the land of the living to the land of the dead," one Ijo senior researcher told us. "If adequate sacrifices are made to them, it is believed that they can return some dying people back to life."

Dead relatives and friends serve as guides to the spirits among the Yoruba. They welcome the spirit in a ritual that is reminiscent of many near-death-experience reports, where loved ones and family members wait at the end of the tunnel and encourage the dying person on. Family members and community chiefs lead newly dead Ijo spirits to the King of the Afterdeath. "Why not make a greeting?" asked one of our informants. "Some living members of the family send messages and gifts to the departed relatives and friends through those who are about to be buried." But family and tribe members are not the only greeters in the realms of possibility. In Hindu and Buddhist paradises, beautiful sensual beings are not so much guides as part of the blissful pleasures—sensual and sexual objects whose accessibility rewards spirits who had maintained self-discipline throughout their lives on earth.

The beauty of these lovely figures leads us to angels. Particularly in the Christian tradition, angels have long served a kind of decorative function, their presence and numbers drawing attention to God's profound holiness. But in earlier traditions angels were messengers, and perhaps the most delightful supposition to come out of the current preoccupation with these winged presences is that they had their origins in the world of birds, which were often seen as accompanying spirits to the afterdeath.

Although angels have been studied, described, charted, and classified for centuries, it was a sixth-century mystic and theologian named Dionysius who came up with the hierarchical system of angels—those angels highest on his order were the closest to God. The higher the level, the more incorporeal the angel; those of lower orders had more physical characteristics.

Here are some of Dionysius's categories:

- Seraphim form the top rank. They, like God, are utterly bodiless. Their name itself means fire or radiance, suggesting the power to blaze up. Seraphim surround the throne of God and have six wings. They are armed with swords.
- Archangels come to earth to announce great events. Gabriel, who signaled the arrival of Christ and who, with his trumpet, will signal the last judgment, was—is—an archangel.
- Cherubim are not necessarily the plump-limbed, winged infants portrayed in late Renaissance paintings, but can actually be much more exotic. As imagined by Ezekiel in the Bible, a single cherubim is composed of four creatures with four heads and four sets of wings—and cloven hooves, like those of calves. According to some writers, cherubim have a significant responsibility in ruling

the universe. They are awesome, dignified, and important creatures.

• Angels called Dominations are concerned with regulating other
  angels. Aspiring to true lordship, they carry scepters and orbs as
  emblems of their authority.[11]

The modern enthusiasm for angels brings with it another form of
angel classification: according to their area of expertise. Thus, Gabriel, Raphael, and Michael are all angels concerned with love, and
Michael and Raphael deal with miracles as well. For mercy, we took
to Tadhial; for patience, Oriphial; for optimism, Verchiel.[12]

All angels are winged. And here is a lovely thing about those wings:
angels don't need to flap them; their thoughts and desires alone are
able to move the wings to take them where they want to go.[13]

THE VISIONARIES

The shamans of tribal cultures are the designated emissaries into the
unknown, and rigorous training precedes their piercing of its borders.
In the past decade, we have read much of such imaginal travels as they
occur in tribal cultures, and in recent years many people in the West
have yearned for and sought out shamanic wisdom that might apply
to their own destiny, both in life and after death.

But the West has its own visionary travelers, those who sense,
perceive, and see the possibilities beyond death. Here is a sampling of
Western visions from the cornucopia of global afterdeath images.

Emanuel Swedenborg

Never has there been so prolific and minutely expressive a living
observer of the afterdeath as the eighteenth-century mystic Emanuel
Swedenborg. Master of an amazing array of talents, in middle age he
achieved deep trance states during which he visited the afterdeath,

communicated with the dead, and then brought back detailed reports of the realms beyond death.

By the end of his life, Swedenborg had filled twenty volumes with such reports. Fascinatingly, looked at now, his descriptions resemble contemporary reports to an amazing degree: In both we find minute depictions of the passage through a dark tunnel, the presence of welcoming spirits, fabulous landscapes free of time and space, a dazzling light emitting the essence of love, and a life review process that all newly arrived spirits undergo. However, particularly interesting and detailed are Swedenborg's reports of "thought balls," which angels used instead of language to communicate.

As to Swedenborg's belief in the possibilities he describes, his assertions are unambiguous: "Everything that I have written is as true as you now behold me," he wrote. "I might have said much more had it been permitted to me. After death you will see it all, and then we shall have much to say to each other on the subject."[14]

Rudolf Steiner

Rudolf Steiner was an occult philosopher and literary scholar of the late nineteenth and early twentieth centuries (1861–1925). In his vast writings, he was as comfortable and apparently knowledgeable in discussing life beyond death and the return through embryonic life in a mother's womb as he was in developing innovations in medicine, education, architecture, drama, agriculture, and art. Steiner crossed boundaries as if they weren't there. To him, any such excursion—for example, from life into the afterdeath and back again via embryonic life—was an exploration of the spirit's growth and its participation in the evolution of the universe. His most fascinating and (vitally) imaginative descriptions involved afterdeath travels to distant planets.[15]

Terence McKenna

Among the most powerful Western afterdeath visions come to us from contemporary Terence McKenna, ethnobotanist and author of *Food of the Gods: The Search for the Original Tree of Knowledge.*

McKenna used the chemical dimethyltryptamine [DMT] to travel to other worlds, ones he likens to the afterdeath.

DMT is a hallucinogen that alters the visual capacities and, as McKenna puts it, "gives tremendous permission for the imagination." He contends that the drug shows us what is waiting on another side, and that many people who have taken the same dosage independently have reported precisely the same perceptions.

"You burst into space," he says. "Somehow, you don't know how, you can tell it's underground and an immense weight is above it. You have a feeling of enclosure, and yet the space itself is open. It is warm. It is comfortable . . . [and] there is no ambiguity about the fact that there are entities . . . there."[16]

These entities, as McKenna describes them, are bejeweled balls, self-propelled, the size of basketballs, but as beautiful and most reminiscent of huge Faberge eggs (and of Swedenborg's thought balls). These globes move quickly and change rapidly. They wait for us to appear and cheer us lovingly when we do. "Do not give way to astonishment!" they exhort us. "Do not give way to amazement!" But we *are* astonished. When these globe-beings speak, their words are visible—complex geometric forms. And we perceive their meaning with our eyes.

What the balls convey is the interconnectedness of reality. This idea is expressed in many ways and the result in this psychedelic heaven is a continual and building awareness of wholeness and integration. No reward or punishment invades the paradise of the Faberge eggs. Instead, the overriding emotion is joy, a profound happiness on the part of the visitor at suddenly and with certainty apprehending a glimpse of the connectedness of all things.

Each of these three men have delivered up distinct visions of the possible. How many more visions might we collect from around the world?

REFLECTIONS ON THE STAGE OF POSSIBILITIES

I have had many wonderful conversations with friends, acquaintances, and clients about the rich and colorful afterdeath sites described in this chapter and how sharply they contrast with other limited visions of the destinations of the dead. I've watched people in grief who have wondered "Where is she now?" grow fascinated and hopeful at a description of the Buddhist journey in the Bardo stage or of Hindu wish-cows in a beautiful paradise ready to reward newly arrived spirits with their most personal desires.[17]

That the dead are *someplace,* though, is the most reassuring concept of all. This idea counteracts the fearsome image of a tiny, lonely spirit whirling through space into oblivion. The very notion of travel toward a destination in the afterdeath carries with it a sense of unbroken reality—of moving with intention, energy, and perhaps even joy through a mosaic of possibilities.

CHAPTER 6

☙

Stage IV: Return

A Return . . . Imagined

*He must leave. Already earthly emotion is flooding his being, and he is
awash with deep feeling. He doesn't want to go—and yet he is drawn by
curiosity for the new life he will lead and is shaking with excitement at the
change. He wonders, in the most earthly way, if a mistake might not have
been made. Surely he has paid enough—if only he could remember—to be
swallowed upward into the Greater Being.*

*But there is no resistance, no arguing . . . nothing to argue against.
There is only the anticipation of being propelled into his new existence. He
guesses and hopes that there will be a moment just at the beginning when
he will know he is on the way—and then obliteration: All that he knows
now about the interstices between lives will disappear, and he will enter a
living being in an earthly woman's womb.*

*So be it. So it probably has been for himself, he supposes, many times
before. Stopping here between lives has been an existence full of joy and
beauty. To desire that the memory stay with him is only proof of his need
to return to life again.*

*He wishes so ardently that he could take with him just a touch, just a
shred, just a vague intimation of the humming music that is communication
here. In fact, his wishing for it has become unbearable, his anger is really
very sharp when he thinks what he must give up, his sense of the
unfairness of it all seems to be taking him over completely . . . and
he is gone.*

Destinations need not be permanent. Journeys need not be unidirectional. The possibilities open to travelers after death need not capture and hold them forever. For many cultures of the world, the afterdeath journey is not an arc inscribed from departure point to destination, but a circle. Implied in the leaving is the return; contained in death is the seed of rebirth. It is true that the circular journey is often incomplete—the trajectory more like a sphere—the traveler returns to a new place and as a different individual. In this way the possible realms of reality are increased beyond measure: Not only does the spirit travel through untold landscapes in the afterdeath, but it returns to an infinite variety of experiences in life.

Josie

Although I've worked with children in special schools over the years, I've never treated them in my private psychotherapy practice; I haven't been set up for it. There are things you need—toys, dollhouses, art supplies, and so forth—and a lot of books you need to have read. It has been a long time since I've read those books, and my office contains little that a child might like except perhaps pencils and a pad. Besides, I never had the inclination for treating children in one-to-one psychotherapy. But I made an exception—once, only one "two-week" exception as a favor to a client—for Josie.

Josie's mother, Gwendolyn, was my client, and terribly agitated about her twelve-year-old daughter. In brief, the seemingly healthy, well-adjusted girl had suddenly had a psychotic break and had, over the course of several evenings, spun completely out of control. With a hammer, muttering and screaming and physically unstoppable, Josie eventually damaged most of the furniture in the house. Her parents had little choice but to institutionalize her for what they hoped would be a brief stay. But before Gwendolyn approached me with her request, Josie had been hospitalized in a private psychiatric facility for a long six months.

Now, after many fits and starts, Josie was coming home, but as luck would have it, after a string of postponements, she was finally to be released during the very week that her new psychiatrist was leaving on a long-planned trip. Her mother was overwhelmed with urgent commitments to *her* mother, Josie's grandmother. "If you could only be a backup," Gwendolyn begged me. "See Josie, keep her grounded, just talk with her a little until her psychiatrist comes back. It's such a bad time."

"Absolutely not!" I responded. Professionally and personally I was completely unprepared to play that role. Working with children takes a lot out of you—and there was no way I could add Josie to an already full practice. It was one of those requests you don't even think about. Would I put my head in a lion's mouth or go over Niagara Falls in a barrel? The answer was no.

Then I had a dream. I was fishing with my father and caught a great big fish. As I unhooked it, I found that my hook had gone not only into the big fish but into another, smaller fish inside. The larger one was really just an encasement, a protection, for the smaller fish. The meaning of this dream seemed too obvious to me and not something I wanted to accept, so, assuming there was something I was missing, I consulted a Jungian colleague about the dream. After asking me what was going on in my life and my practice, her opinion was unshakable: "It looks like Josie is your client whether you want her or not. It really is a very strong dream, Sukie." And so Josie became my client.

Working with this young girl was the challenge of my career. Scared, bright, funny, and very difficult, Josie was disoriented and seemingly as unfathomable as the patients at Bellevue I had worked with as a summer volunteer when I was sixteen. Still, we got along well. Though relentlessly confused, Josie never missed a session (much to my amazement), and although she always destroyed my Kleenex boxes, scattering wads of paper everywhere, and though in the beginning she never, ever, looked at me, I felt we somehow connected.

Being unable to explain what was going on between us and barely able to conceptualize well what should be going on while I worked with Josie, I constantly consulted with psychiatrists and psychopharmacologists, social workers, and specialists in childhood disorders. I sought advice from any informed professionals who might give me some insight into how best to help this child. There was a missing piece somewhere and I couldn't find it: According to Gwendolyn,

Josie had had a pretty normal development, the family was basically healthy, no traumatic or unusual events preceded the break, and tests showed Josie to be neurologically normal—but still, a piece of the puzzle was missing. Focus on Gwendolyn, said my consultants, and I did. Consider the father; I did. Observe your own dreams; I did that. And Josie's dreams, which of course I did. Everything helped, but a mystery remained. And all the while I wondered what this child was doing in my adult practice.

But I was fascinated, compelled—and enchanted. There were things about Josie: She was miserable and frightened, but she was funny, too. She was a fabulous, intuitive artist. She was red-haired and a little plump. Interesting, I thought, concerned that I was overidentifying with my patient: I myself am considered funny, am a great art lover and have a folk art collection, and am red-haired and ever verging on plump. We both loved to eat, and as time went on and Josie became healthier, we would spend our sessions "breaking the rules" by going out for hot fudge sundaes or talking intensely over bagels and cream cheese. In the evenings, breaking more rules—this time those that separated my practice from my private life—I took frantic, agitated, long, long phone calls from Josie, who in many ways had lost most of her basic social skills and was having a hard time relating to the students at her new, special school.

"What do I do when someone says 'hi'?" she would ask in a typical nine P.M. conversation.

"You say 'hi' back," I'd respond, trying to be as concrete as she was.

"Do I smile when I say it?"

"If you like the person, you smile. You smile according to how much you like the person."

"But how do I know how much I like the person, Sukie?"

So it would go, an evening's heart-felt questions. Josie was a fast learner, and once a basic crisis was settled she would incorporate the answers easily. Until the next evening, when she'd call to find out, "How do I walk down the street with somebody, Sukie?" In many ways she was like a much smaller child who had to be raised again and rapidly before too much time was lost.

Gwendolyn seemed happy and relieved at the strength of the connection between Josie and me, and the agreed-upon two weeks gave way to months. I was utterly mystified at myself. What was with me? I had always held by the set of rules by which I defined my practice. Was I indulging myself somehow in this case? And if so, why? I couldn't answer these questions—and I couldn't send Josie away to another therapist. She was making good progress—albeit two steps forward and one step back—and she seemed to find a kind of comfort in our relationship and in some deep way to thrive, something that was confirmed by the psychologist and teachers at her school.

I continued to consult experts of every stripe, and one day decided to go somewhat far afield to meet with Michael Lutin, an astrologer whom I had never met but of whom friends spoke highly. I thought he might be able to draw up an astrological chart of Josie to determine the influences under which she had been born, something that might give me some insight into her inherent problems and strengths. But after hearing my story, as well as Josie's, Michael asked me a surprising question: "Sukie, what were you doing six months before to six months after Josie was born?"

It came into my mind like a rocket: Twelve years ago I had had a miscarriage. My husband and I had been terribly disappointed at having lost the baby. It was something we hadn't anticipated at all, and it came as a shock from left field.

"I was having a miscarriage," I whispered in answer to Michael's unexpected question, chilled by the intensity of the memory. Michael and I sat in silence for as long as I could stand it. "So, what are you thinking, Michael?" I finally asked.

"Sukie," he said gently, "perhaps Josie is your lost child."

Something clutched at my chest. I could hardly breathe. I pondered, wondered, considered. Finally, from somewhere deep inside, an unhealed place, I cried.

Michael Lutin was the last expert-consultant I engaged to help me with Josie. After having seen him, I felt I had my missing piece. I continued to treat Josie, allowing now the joy and love I felt for her to be integrated into our work—not left outside the door as I had been doing so scrupulously before. One day about a year after I had seen Michael, Josie asked me if I was her mother. "You know better than that," I responded, alert and concerned that we were dealing here with more than psychoanalytic transference, in which being seen as the mother (and other important figures) was a goal over time. "I know," she responded, "but I mean, like, kind of a make-believe mother for a while? More before, when I was really sick. You know," she said. "Yeah, well, kind of," was all I was capable of answering.

In the end, I wound up treating Josie for three years, going from every day to twice-a-week sessions to once-a-week sessions. She grew tall; I am short. Her nose took on a new shape and, the punk era having dawned, she began dyeing her red hair green. The resemblances between us faded, and Josie got better and was well on her way to a successful adulthood. One day in the course of her regular session she announced in her forthright manner, "I've outgrown you, Sukie. I need to talk with someone who treats grownups now." And our time together was over.

What on earth had Michael Lutin been suggesting?

Simply that Josie's body might have been the casement, the new "house," for a particular spirit returned from the afterdeath—a human who had once existed in another body but who had died, in this case before birth. He was saying that Josie could have been my daughter reborn, come back to complete unfinished business with the world of the living and, specifically, with me.

Many would consider Michael Lutin's suggestion that Josie was the reincarnation of my unborn child to be an outrageous remark, too far out, incredible. But for many people in many cultures, his suggestion would have not only made perfect sense but would have rung true and explained a lot about Josie's troubles and our subsequent relationship. For many people around the world, return is taken for granted.

That one reincarnates after every physical death is basic in the Igbo belief system of West Africa. . . . The Igbo man says:

> *When I come back to earth,*
> *I shall be a big man or woman!*

When I come back to earth,
I will never again be
A native of this town

When I come back to earth
I shall not be a merciful person

When I come back to earth
I shall be a scholar.

Coming seven times to this earth
or eight times more,

I will never again be a native of this town.

"In the olden days," writes an expert on the Igbo culture, "as soon as a child is born, the fortune teller is invited to divine which ancestor has come back into the family. . . . As soon as the correct name is divined, a welcome sacrifice involving a ram for a male ancestor—a hen or a she-goat for a female ancestor—is performed. Certain types of ancestors (e.g., warriors) would return to the spirit world (die) after causing the family a lot of hardship if this ceremony is not performed soon after their re-birth."[1]

"My mother died in 1981," a Yoruban senior researcher told us, "and the following year my wife gave birth to that girl you see outside the house. She takes much after my mother—so much so that we named her Iyabo, which means, 'Mother Comes Back.' " To the Yoruban family noting the resemblance, Iyabo was not simply a child who resembled her grandmother; the spirit within the body *was* the grandmother.

On another visit in Africa, my Western expectations clashed with Nigerian realities when Edmundo and I were invited to an elegant meal at the home of a well-known professor. "Ah, here comes father," the man announced as we were having drinks, and we all stood up, expecting, judging from the professor's age, a frail old man in his eighties. Into the room scampered a three-year-old, full of energy and curiosity. My host, noticing my confusion, showed me a mark on his son's forehead— a little mark, to be sure—and explained that his father had had the very same mark in the same place. "He is a part of all our family meetings, all our decision making, sitting where my father sat. He *is* my father," he told me. "The return of the spirits who leave us through death is not a concept as you would call it," said the professor, "but a reality in our lives. They leave and they return. It is a cycle."

All over the world, spirits are reborn. In some South American groups, for instance, shamans preside at births. In the Makuna group, it is the shaman's job to guide a grandparent's soul from the house of the dead in the afterdeath into its new house, the newborn's body.[2] In other groups, midwives help with this transfer. Among these people, midwives are not merely birth attendants; they are, in a hands-on way, guides in the journey across the border into life.[3]

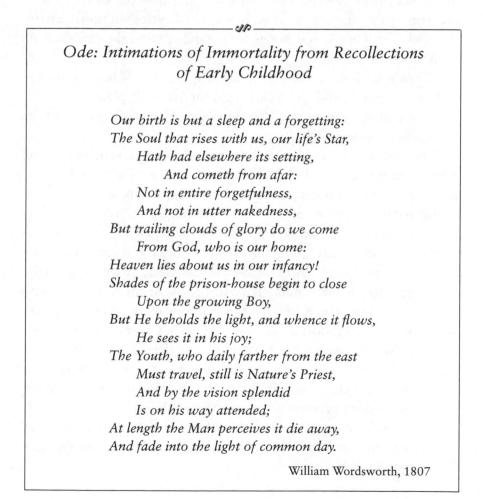

Ode: Intimations of Immortality from Recollections of Early Childhood

Our birth is but a sleep and a forgetting:
The Soul that rises with us, our life's Star,
Hath had elsewhere its setting,
And cometh from afar:
Not in entire forgetfulness,
And not in utter nakedness,
But trailing clouds of glory do we come
From God, who is our home:
Heaven lies about us in our infancy!
Shades of the prison-house begin to close
Upon the growing Boy,
But He beholds the light, and whence it flows,
He sees it in his joy;
The Youth, who daily farther from the east
Must travel, still is Nature's Priest,
And by the vision splendid
Is on his way attended;
At length the Man perceives it die away,
And fade into the light of common day.

William Wordsworth, 1807

Among a particular group of Australian Aborigines called the Yongu, not shamans or midwives but clouds are the medium for the passage of spirits. When spirits are released from the body at death, they rise up from the ground as clouds and drift across the sky until they come down again as rain. The rainwater enters the watercourses and rivers, and the spirits within it become part of rocks that surround people's wells and the sacred objects that the people place at the bottom of those wells. Without their knowledge, women who pump, wash in, or drink the water, conceive—that is, the spirits in the water, wells, and rocks enter their bodies as new children. In this way, spirits once housed in living bodies on earth become reborn into others. For the Yongu, then, rebirth is not only as natural as the eternal water cycle on earth; it is part of the web of natural cycles within which we live and die.[4] One Yoruban senior researcher cited the evidence all around:

"When you plant maize, it germinates and grows. When the corn is ripe, you harvest, and the following year you still plant the seeds, which eventually germinate. This shows you that there is a return to this earth by all who die.

"The return to this earth is demonstrated too by the sun, moon, and some other heavenly bodies. In the morning, the sun rises, but it sets in the evening, only to re-rise the following morning. The moon is up for fourteen days and then keeps away for fourteen days before resurfacing on the human sphere again. So is human experience."

In many cultures the spirit is in no way a strictly human phenomenon. One report came from Dr. Maria Paradiso, an anthropologist who studies the Krenar Indian tribe of Brazil. At the time we spoke, some years ago, the Krenars' homeland was threatened by the wreckage of the rainforest, and only ninety-six members remained. Dr. Paradiso told me that the Krenars believe that human beings have seven souls, though only one, the one you bring with you when you are born, is the major soul. At death, spirits in the forest capture the main soul, and the person dies (if any of the other souls are captured, the person falls ill). At that time, the other six souls are set free—yet the person will not be peaceful until the main soul, the one that has been captured, is liberated.

"How is that done?" I asked. "How is the captured soul freed?"

"It must be fed. The living must place food on the grave for many years. The soul will come there to eat, and eventually the spirits that hold the soul will be satisfied and will let the soul go.

"However, if the spirits are *not* satisfied—if the food laid out is insufficient or the grave is poorly tended—the captive soul will become a panther, and not a peaceful panther but one destined to attack the community. So you see," she told me, "the Krenar live in great fear of this animal. This is the way the Krenars see death: as a panther that attacks the community."

Far back in time and half a world away, the belief among the ancient Greeks that human spirits can transmigrate into animals led some to practice vegetarianism. They prohibited the eating of animal bodies on the chance that those bodies might be inhabited by human souls. An even more extreme view held that the same might be true of fruits and vegetables—which meant that although such believers might subsist on fruits and vegetables, they refused to cut up such foodstuffs themselves, but consigned that task to believers of a lower rank. Eating a green pepper apparently seemed neutral enough, but no one wanted to be the one to bite into its soul.[5]

THE MAHAPATRA'S STORY

In many tribal cultures, there is no return to earth; people slip across and are gone from life on earth forever. In some groups only the "good" return, and only those who have had a "good" death—meaning a timely, natural one marked by burial rituals executed carefully by the mourners—have the opportunity to return. In others the return is based on having been "bad," having failed to contribute all one could have, and having left unfinished business, such as murder.

In the Hindu and Buddhist religious traditions, the concept of karma adds complexity, as well as drama and suspense, to the process of rebirth. How souls return, where they return, if they return, and into which bodies and circumstances depend on the person's past behavior. In these highly developed and fascinating traditions, the Wheel of Life goes round and round, and not until all consequences of past lives have been dealt with are we liberated and released. In the Hindu tradition, all earthly desires and, in the Buddhist view, freedom from all illusion, permit us to slip off the Wheel of Life to become part of the greater, more profound reality.

Karma changes everything. With karma determining the kind of life one will live next time, there is no question of going back into similar existences. Instead, the person who leads a good life will be rewarded with a comfortable existence next time. An evil person will be punished with a hard life of misery—and no one, no deity, will be to blame. Paradoxically, the system can be seen as an ultimate expression of personal responsibility.

"The goal is to keep from returning," the Indian Mahapatra told us as he paused in his rituals for attending the dead, "but most people are so bogged down in their karma that they cannot escape it. Therefore, another life is the immediate destination, and rest or cessation the ultimate goal. . . . One major image comes from the Bhagavad-Gita, in which Krishna explains . . . that the soul casts off and puts on bodies as a man might take off old clothes and put on new ones. He goes on to explain that the soul is immortal—fire cannot burn it, water cannot wet it, weapons cannot cut it. Bodies get destroyed, but the soul is indestructible and carries on from life to life until it is released and goes to god."

The Mahapatra's minute description of the death process and its interrelationship with a return to life only highlights the complexity of every individual's fate:

When Yamaraj comes to take one's life, the first thing he does is to grab the person's feet. Then he starts trying to extract the *prana* [life, or life breath] by gradually moving up the leg toward the head region. He beats the *prana* to make it come with him. There is a lot of pain involved in the process of dying. The *prana* tries to escape Yamaraj and flees upward to lodge itself in the chest as a last stand.

From there, if it succeeds in reaching the head region, it can escape via any of the orifices there—for example, mouth, nostrils, ears, eyes, or, if the person is so fortunate, through the skull. If not, it has to escape via the anus, which means that the traveler will have to go to hell.

If *prana* escapes via the skull, it means ... the traveler will not have to return to this earth in any form. There is a jellylike substance in the skull that is the repository of intelligence and sensibility. It is through this that a person makes a distinction of what is good or bad. It is when this jelly bursts in the process of dying, spontaneously, that the solar route becomes available to the traveler. ... Death by any other orifice makes available to the *prana* the lunar route—and, in this case, the person has to return to earth.

Indian mystic philosopher Sri Aurobindo contributes a sense of the changes that take place once the return is set in motion: "A new life is not a taking up of the development exactly where it stopped in the last, it does not merely repeat and continue our past surface personality and formation of nature. There is an assimilation, a discarding and strengthening and rearrangement of the old characters and motives, a new ordering of the development of the past and a selection for purposes of the future without which the new start cannot be fruitful or carry forward the evolution. For each birth is a new start; it develops indeed from the past, but is not a mechanical continuation; rebirth is not a constant reiteration but a progression, it is the machinery of an evolutionary process."[6] There is a "mechanics" to reincarnation, Aurobindo tells us, whereby the soul on its journey changes and evolves.

It can seem cruel and relentless, this complicated and anxiety-producing repetition, this continuous experience the indestructible soul must have of the consequences of his or her behavior in life. But the Mahapatra attempts to show the justice in the system. "You observe a disparity in society," he says. "One person works very hard but is barely able to make a living, whereas another leads an easy life. This disparity can be traced to their karma in past lives. In other words, karma serves as an explanation for a world that might seem to a nonbeliever horribly unjust, miserably unfair." If hard times befell you and you were trying as hard as you could to live a good life, it might well comfort you to believe that there were reasons for your miseries—even if you couldn't remember, across the span of time and death, what those reasons were.

FINDING THE DALAI LAMA

Among the Tibetan Buddhists, reincarnation has one unique function not found in other groups: securing the transmission of the leadership of the spiritual faith. Because the priestly elite is usually celibate, it cannot produce its own high priest. Instead, when the spiritual leader, the Dalai Lama, dies, a party of priests specially trained in the search go out into the country to seek the baby into whom the spirit of the leader has passed.

In his book *My Land and My People,* the current Dalai Lama describes how, as a toddler, he was tracked down in his idyllic home, on a farm, to become His Holiness, the spiritual leader of Tibet. Special priests followed clues as to where the spirit of the late Dalai Lama would reincarnate: "It was recalled that after the Dalai Lama died, his body was placed . . . facing toward south but after a few days it was seen that the face had turned to the northeast . . . on the northeast side of the shrine where the body sat, a great star-shaped fungus suddenly appeared. This and other evidence indicated the direction where the new Dalai Lama should be sought."

A regent traveled to a sacred lake, one famous for the visions it produced, and there, after many days of meditation, he saw a vision of "a monastery with roofs of jade green and gold and a house with turquoise tiles. Detailed description of these visions was written down and kept as a strict secret."7

Following the regent's meditation, wise men traveled to the village identified in the vision and found the turquoise-tiled house. A little boy, then two years old, lived there with his large family. Untaught, this boy called the people in the search party—whom he had never met before—by their names and instinctively reached for items held close by the previous Dalai Lama. When the party was preparing to leave, the little boy insisted on going with them . . . and became the fourteenth Dalai Lama, so visible now as the loving leader of his refugee people, untiring in his efforts to keep Tibetan Buddhism alive and vital despite its treatment by the Chinese.

THOSE WHO BELIEVE

Judaism, Christianity, Islam, and other monotheistic religions never formally embraced the concept of a personal reincarnation. But the disavowal of the notion of rebirth by institutional religions has done nothing to dissuade many great thinkers in these traditions from considering reincarnation a concept as natural and credible as those of Heaven and Hell—perhaps more so.

Plato, for example, wove reincarnation into his beautiful and detailed descriptions of the moral universe: "O youth of young man, who fancy that you are neglected by the Gods, know that if you become worse you shall go to the worse souls, or if better to the better . . . this is the justice of heaven, which neither you nor any other unfortunate will ever glory in escaping."[8] In our Western intellectual history, Plato's reality has served for centuries as a touchstone for rationality, and threaded through his writings is a depiction of the Wheel of Life remarkably similar to those so vividly functioning in the Hindu and Buddhist traditions.

Fast forward many centuries to take note of other familiar individuals' responses to the concept of reincarnation:

- *Benjamin Franklin* "Finding myself to exist in the world, I believe I shall in some shape or other always exist; and, with all the inconveniences human life is liable to, I shall not object to a new edition of mine, hoping, however, that the *errata* of the last may be corrected." [From the *Letters*]

- *Walt Whitman* "I know I am deathless. No doubt I have died myself ten thousand times before." [From *Leaves of Grass*]
- *Carl Jung* "I could well imagine that I might have lived in former centuries and there encountered questions I was not yet able to answer; that I had to be born again because I had not fulfilled the task that was given to me. When I die, my deeds will follow along with me—that is how I imagine it. I will bring with me what I have done. In the meantime it is important to insure that I do not stand at the end with empty hands." [From *Memories, Dreams, and Reflections*]
- *William Butler Yeats* "Many times man lives and dies. . . . / Whether man dies in his bed / Or the rifle knocks him dead, / A brief parting from those dear / Is the worst man has to fear." [From *Under Ben Bulben*]

These quotations, and many more from Western thinkers, were compiled by Joseph Head and S. L. Cranston, in a book titled *Reincarnation*.[9] I found this gathering of quotes years after I had seen Michael Lutin, but was struck with how they bore witness to the utter naturalness and deep attractiveness of the concept of rebirth, even for those deeply steeped in Western, and especially Christian, traditions.

Spirits never die, as we are told, but return and return until they cast off their bindings to join the greater reality. These joyful and optimistic words from the *Bhagavad-Gita,* the great book of the Hindu journey, imbue with familiarity the cycle of death and rebirth:

The wise in heart mourn not for those that live, nor those that die. Never the spirit was born; the spirit shall cease to be never. Never was time it was not. End and Beginning are dreams! Death hath not touched it at all, dead though the house of it seems! Nay, as when one layeth his worn-out robes away, and, taking new ones, sayeth, "These will I wear today!" so putteth by the spirit lightly its garb of flesh, and passeth to inherit a residence afresh.[10]

"A residence afresh"! The phrase makes a striking contrast to the description of that darkened room whose door slams forever, the room that symbolizes death for those who face it with fear and trembling.

"We only come to dream, we only come to sleep;
It is not true, it is not true
That we come to live on Earth."

"Where are we to go from here?
We came here only to be born,
As our home is beyond,
Where the fleshless abide."

"Perchance, does anyone really live on Earth?
The Earth is not forever, but just to remain a short while."

The Day of the Dead, a Mexican Tradition

Translated from an unknown poet by Angel Maria Garibay
and Michakle Leon Portilla

The concept of return is so potent that even Judaism, Christianity, and Islam, while rejecting individual rebirths, advance the idea of a collective rebirth, or group resurrection, of their people. For the Jews, when the Messiah comes, the dead will rise. In Christianity, Christ's resurrection signals a second life for the son of God. In Islam, there is a "second death," when the body and soul are resurrected for a brief time after death while judgment occurs; then death recurs. However, on the last day of time, as with the Jews, all bodies will arise.

It is a rare culture in which death is utterly final and the human spirit is obliterated with no promise of a return. The concept of a group rebirth reflects an unchallengeable confidence in the immortality of the soul, and this confidence in turn represents an irrepressible hopefulness, a celebration of a universe that permits no permanent destruction, but that gives evidence of change, of transformation. To admit the possibility of rebirth and return is to step away from fear.

REMEMBERING

While the concept of reincarnation might be an inherently optimistic idea, the return to life—the laying away of the worn-out robes and taking on new ones—is not necessarily an inherently joyful experience. Witness Josie, whose suffering was what brought her to me in the first place. Within the context of karma, returning spirits may have to enter new lives of terrible misery and suffering. Further, esoteric schools teach that being born is far more excruciating than dying. Having found a closer union with God, or with one's true community, or having finally discovered the meaning of one's existence, why return? Few, these teachings say, actually want to.

If the idea of return is accurate, if we do indeed don new lives as we don new suits of clothes, why can't we remember our past lives?

As with any persistent idea that remains stubbornly unverifiable, the perspectives on reincarnation form a vast spectrum, ranging from the superficial to the scrupulously empirical. Some scholars of reincarnation teach that it is possible, although not ordinary, that we *can* remember our past lives, and a large measure of energy, talent, and work has gone into explaining how this takes place.

Ian Stevenson is a psychiatrist at the University of Virginia who has established research guidelines for studying past-life remembrances. His work has been heralded by skeptics as well as believers as reliable, scientific, and informative. He studies those who remember—or who seem to remember—past lives. His goal is not simply to verify the possibility of reincarnation itself, but also to explain unusual behavior and even medical phenomena (such as congenital disorders and birthmarks) that so far defy other explanations. Among the behaviors and patterns of the psyche Stevenson identifies as possibly explained by

reincarnation are some of our most stubborn and mystifying psychological puzzles:

- unusual appetites and untaught skills in early childhood;
- unusual interests and types of childhood play;
- addictions and cravings;
- casts of temperament;
- precocious sexuality;
- gender-identity confusion.

However, our ability to tap directly into the substratum of rebirth
material is far from our reach at the moment. Discovering and *verify-
ing* the reports of true "rememberers" other than by intuition or
instinct is a painstaking effort requiring the training and discipline of a
scientific sleuth. In tracking down the leads that come to him from all
over the world, Stevenson relies on a cadre of psychological and
parapsychological researchers. He studies children almost exclusively
and employs dedicated adults as his detectives in checking out the
leads. Both children and parents are extensively interviewed as are
teachers, neighbors, doctors—anyone who might have heard the child
give evidence of memories, however imperfect, of past lives. Stevenson's four-volume *Cases of the Reincarnation Type* report on cases in
India, Lebanon, Turkey, Thailand, Burma, and Sri Lanka.

"In studying cases, I have to use the methods of the historian,
lawyer and psychiatrist. I gather testimony from as many witnesses as
possible. It is not uncommon for me to interview twenty-five people in
one case of reincarnation. And I have frequently gone back to interview the same person several years later. . . . I have first to eliminate
the possibility of fraud."[11] He must also rule out casual exposures to
the facts or observations claimed to be reincarnation memories.

Bongkuch Promsin

Stevenson's case histories are too lengthy to be fully presented here,
but the case of Bongkuch Promsin illustrates the kinds of material he
works with. As soon as he was old enough to speak, Bongkuch, a child

in Thailand, began to report that he was the reincarnation of an individual named Chamrat, who had been murdered in a village nine kilometers from his current home village. Bongkuch described an array of information about the personality of Chamrat and his family and described where he himself had been after Chamrat's death. This, he said, was near a bamboo bush close to the site of the murder. Bongkuch lived nearby for seven years. One day, during a rainstorm, as he told it, Bongkuch saw his current father and followed him home on a bus.

Bongkuch's father could indeed remember going by bus to the very village named and coming home in the rain. And this was shortly before his wife became pregnant with Bongkuch.[12] The timing, concepts, and personality descriptions, all so atypical of the interests of a very young child, were a starting point to Stevenson, who approaches such material with the objectivity of an empirical scientist.

Stevenson's work comes closest to giving us clear, firm evidence that rebirth is factual. Other past-lives explorers, however, are more focused on the potential for the concept of reincarnation to heal psychological wounds and eliminate psychic and physiological pain.

Dr. Roger Woolger is a psychologist who uses "regression therapy" in an attempt both to shed light on and relieve his clients' unexplained psychological and physiological symptoms. Employing hypnosis and other measures, Woolger urges his clients to travel back in time into possible past existences. Here the operative word is *possible,* for, in contrast to Dr. Stevenson's work, Roger Woolger's does not focus on the reality of those existences; instead, Woolger suggests that uncovering and exploring past lives even as metaphors have their own psychotherapeutic value. If a client tells a past-life story full of details that relate to and even explain current problems, and if those explanations bring relief, Dr. Woolger considers the question of whether or not the story is true to be irrelevant. "I never encourage my clients to investigate the historical background of a past-life memory, since this can drain energy from the immediate power of the image or story that is emerging."[13]

ঞ৯

Rules for Being Human

1. You will receive a body.
   You may like it or hate it, but it will be yours for the entire period this time around.
2. You will learn lessons.
   You are enrolled in a full-time informal school called life. Each day in this school you will have the opportunity to learn lessons. You may like the lessons or think them irrelevant and stupid.
3. There are no mistakes, only lessons.
   Growth is a process of trial and error, experimentation. The "failed" experiments are as much a part of the process as the experiment that ultimately "works."
4. A lesson is repeated until learned.
   A lesson will be presented to you in various forms until you have learned it. When you have learned it, you can then go on to the next lesson.
5. Learning lessons does not end.
   There is no part of life that does not contain its lessons. If you are alive, there are lessons to be learned.
6. "There" is no better than "here."
   When your "there" has become a "here" you will simply obtain another "there" that will, again, look better than "here."
7. Others are merely mirrors of you.
   You cannot love or hate something about another person unless it reflects to you something you love or hate about yourself.
8. What you make of life is up to you.
   You have all the tools and resources you need. What you do with them is up to you. The choice is yours.
9. Your answers lie inside you.
   The answers to life's questions lie inside you. All you need to do is look, listen, and trust.
10. You will forget all this.

Anonymous

Woolger tells this story of one of his subjects.

Winifred was a middle-aged woman who had had chronic sinusitis since her early life. During [a past-lives workshop] she relived the lonely death on a battlefield during World War I of a young man who had grown up in London as an orphan. The young man had made friends for the first time in the trenches during the campaign. When he suddenly found himself choking on mustard gas, in the middle of a surprise attack, he realized momentarily, as he lay dying, how much he was about to lose in terms of his newly found friendships. But the gas blocked any possibility to weep and grieve. When Winifred relived this experience, she was able to realize how much grief the young man had never expressed and was at last able to let it go. Almost miraculously, her sinuses unblocked. And when she came back to a later session in the workshop, she reported that she had woken up that particular morning for the first time in over twenty years able to breath through her sinuses.[14]

Another investigator into remembrance is Dr. Brian Weiss, Chairman of the Department of Psychiatry at Mt. Sinai Medical Center in Miami Beach, Florida, a graduate of the Yale University Medical School, and chief resident in Yale's Department of Psychiatry. Clearly, as his background indicates, Dr. Weiss has had many encouragements to take the mainstream position, but one particular psychiatric patient brought him slowly to the view that remembering past lives could potentially facilitate psychological healing. In his book *Many Masters, Many Lives,* Weiss tells the story of his patient, Catherine, who came to him seeking relief from years of anxiety, panic attacks, and phobias. Her symptoms had been with her since childhood, but in adulthood they became much worse; when she sought help from Weiss, she was becoming more emotionally paralyzed every day, so much so that she was nearly unable to function.[15]

Writes Weiss, "Years of disciplined study trained my mind to think as a scientist and as a physician, molding me along the narrow paths of conservatism in my profession. I distrusted anything that could not be proven by traditional scientific methods. I was aware of some of the studies in parapsychology that were being conducted at major universities across the country, but they didn't hold my attention. [Reincarnation and regression therapy] all seemed farfetched to me. Then I met Catherine."[16]

For eighteen months, Weiss used standard psychotherapy techniques to treat Catherine, but her symptoms showed no signs of abating. Turning to hypnosis, he took her back through the years of her life, but the sessions turned up nothing that accounted for her symptoms. Then one day Catherine began describing a scene spontaneously that she identified as having occurred in 1863 B.C. "There are trees and a stone road. I see a fire with cooking. My hair is blond. I'm wearing a long brown dress and sandals. I am twenty-five. I have a girl child whose name is Cleastra. . . . She's Rachel. It's very hot." In Catherine's current life, Rachel was Catherine's niece, with whom she was very close.

Weiss, the skeptic, felt as if he had stumbled onto something. He encouraged Catherine to continue telling her stories under hypnosis, and her reincarnation experiences make up the bulk of his book. Weiss reports that he went on to treat others in the same way, carefully taping, evaluating, and validating the material as best he could. "I am still a scientist," he says, and concludes as an informed observer that, as with Catherine, in case after case, "symptoms resolved as the lifetimes unfolded." And, as much to the point in the context of *this* book, in the patients who successfully went through regression therapy with Weiss, "the fear of death diminished."[17]

The work of Rabbi Yonassan Gershom, another researcher into reincarnation, began as many projects do, through a chance meeting. In giving his public lectures on the Kabbala and Jewish esoteric teaching, Rabbi Gershom came across something unexpected: the odd possibility that Jews gassed and burned in the Holocaust were surfacing in the bodies and psyches of non-Jews in the postwar generation. This idea first occurred to him as a wisp, a hint, at one of his lectures, when a member of the audience told him a strange tale. "Ever since childhood," he later reported in his book *Beyond the Ashes*, "the very mention of the Holocaust filled [this woman] with unexplained dread.

Now her sister was doing a research paper on concentration camps and insisted on sharing the material, but she simply could not bear it. . . . As my guest talked, I saw the fear in her deep blue eyes. Then suddenly I felt myself slip into an altered state of consciousness, as I sometimes do when counseling. Superimposed over her beautiful face I saw another visage, thin and emaciated. At the same time I could hear the sound of many voices singing an old Hasidic tune. The effect for me was as if we were moving back and forth between two different periods in time. . . . 'I would like to try something,' I said. 'Let me hum a tune and you tell me if you have ever heard it before.' I began humming . . . and her eyes grew wide with terror. Then she broke down and cried, sobbing that she had 'died' in the Holocaust. The tune was *Ani Maamin,* 'I Believe,' a hymn of faith sung by many thousands of Jews as they entered the gas chambers. She had never, in this life, heard the song before."[18]

From that time forward, Rabbi Gershom found clients drawn to him or referred to him who had a certain profile suggesting Holocaust reincarnations. The most dominant characteristics of this profile are these:

- Childhood nightmares, phobias, and so on, with Holocaust themes not commonly known and not known at all to the person or his or her family. One example, which has surfaced in a number of children Gershom treated, is a phobia—an uncontrollable irrational fear—of black boots.
- A non-Jewish heritage and virtually no contact with Jews or Judaism but nevertheless evidence of compulsions, habits, or other behaviors related to Jewish customs and rituals not particularly familiar to non-Jewish people.
- Or, conversely, a Jewish but distinctly nonreligious heritage and yet an innate grasp of Jewish mysticism—that is, a person who has a "feel" for the Hasidic way, or a Jewish child who is innately more religious than his or her parents.
- A feeling of being "out of place" in the family. This feeling Gershom attributes to the fact that the young returned to life much more quickly than adults—and that many children who died during the Holocaust in effect rushed back into life.

- Born during the baby boom, between 1946 and 1953.
- Frequently, suffering from asthma and other breathing problems and/or eating disorders.
- Has light hair and eyes, and especially the only person in the family to have these characteristics.
- Has an intuitively confirmable sincerity.

Gershom sees his work as liberating the anguish of Holocaust victims whose returning spirits have entered people born a generation after them. It is his belief that such historical suffering does not go away by itself, but demands attention through rebirth and persistent expression. In this way, according to Gershom, are we to understand the profound impact of the traumas woven into human history.

Implicit in Gershom's work is the necessity—and the opportunity, provided by rebirth—to look squarely at the damage we sustain as a society from horribly traumatic events, even if that means we must do our looking a generation or generations hence.

If, in fact, we were conscious of living life after life, we might come close to resembling the Winnebago Indians in their fearless, comfortable, balanced view of death. Here's how Paul Radin describes this view in his classic text, *Primitive Religion:*

[Death] was interpreted as a momentary stumbling involving no loss of consciousness. . . . Birth, puberty, and death were thus, very early, recognized as an unending cycle, in which an individual passed from one level of existence to another. . . . As a biological extinction death had no terrors. . . . It was consequently to be interpreted as simply a temporary cessation of activity just as the period between birth and puberty was to be regarded as an abeyance.[19]

I wish so much that I had had the opportunity to discuss—simply discuss—the possibilities and implications of reincarnation with my anxiety-wracked friend James as he faced his death clutching his money to his chest. I wish we had had the time to wonder, to question, to consider the possibilities without having to insist on whether or not they were facts. Perhaps James would have scoffed and refused to consider the possibility of reincarnation, especially for himself. But perhaps—just for a moment in the anguished weeks before his death—James might have considered the thought that his spirit was indestructible, and that something of himself would survive the death of his body. And maybe, even in a fleeting way, he might have gained some relief from that notion. As with a piece of beautiful art, we need not commit to or even understand the idea embodied in it in order to experience pleasure or inspiration from it. In our exposure to the art alone, the limits on our vital imagination can dissolve or move outward in order to include the new.

FULL CIRCLE

So we have come full circle, back to my office and to Josie. Was she, as Michael Lutin suggested, my unborn daughter returned to this life from the afterdeath? Was there unfinished business between us that explained the deep, compelling attachment we felt for one another— as Josie and Dr. Miller this time—and that kept us connected far beyond what was planned and practical? Was my work with her a product of our many sessions together or of a deeper, older bond? Was our physical resemblance meaningful or just a coincidence? Is there always the possibility of meeting others from another life in order to complete or fix or resolve a long-past situation? Are all those we meet and interact with spirits—friends and foes—from other lives and times?

Although no scientists can answer these questions definitively, some proceed, to great effect, *as if*. Others, from bold thinkers to cautious intuitors, embrace the concept of rebirth as the ultimate optimism, implying and reinforcing as it does the indestructibility and immortality of the spirit. As with all the descriptions of the afterdeath presented here, one cannot hope for absolute proof, but one can be disposed to accept the possibilities. Visionary scientist and writer Stanislaus Grof writes, "So convincing is the evidence in favor of past life influences that one can only conclude that those who refuse to consider this an area worthy of serious study must be either uninformed or excessively narrow-minded."[20]

Shush!

Much of the Old Testament literature is known to be stern and foreboding, a strict rendering of law that permits little whimsy or fantasy. But an evolving body of Jewish folk wisdom has come to us as well from ancient times, and this material is often childlike, funny, and sweet. Though formal Jewish belief in no way embraces the concept of individual reincarnation, this small tale, suitable as a child's bedtime story, takes rebirth for granted and treats its mysteries with a light shrug.

People wonder: If we have lived before, why don't we naturally remember?

People wonder: If we have been in Heaven, why don't we naturally remember?

People wonder: If we have all lived and died before, why don't we naturally remember?

The answer is simple.

Go to the mirror and look at your face, particularly at the space between your nose and lips.

See the little dent? It was made by the archangel Gabriel.

When he sends us from Heaven into life, he puts his finger right under our noses. He makes that little dent to remind us of what he tells us: "Shhhhh," he says. "Where you've been is a secret. Don't tell!"

I was so inclined, with Josie, to accept the possibility of return. The loss of that baby and the future family my former husband and I were envisioning was far too abrupt and wrenching. I longed to know who our child might have been. Even in the earliest stages of pregnancy, I had already begun to speak to her. Though twelve years later the girl who walked into my office was profoundly troubled, her appearance—or reappearance—in my life allowed me to bring to bear all my resources in helping her find her own way through her severe difficulties.

When I think of it now, I consider the opportunity with gratitude. Josie needed a mother; her biological mother was overwhelmed. Furthermore, perhaps, for a while, I needed a daughter. The idea of having the chance to express a thwarted impulse in myself opens my heart; the idea of never having the chance to meet a girl who may have been my lost daughter and give something of myself to her, depresses my spirit, limits my world. Given the choice, I favor the first.

REFLECTIONS ON STAGE IV: RETURN

Reincarnation is a flame that can shine a new light on every aspect of life. Sensing a deeper meaning that extends across the boundary of time can lend fascination to even the most mundane encounter: One's current life can become a poem to study, gloss, and plumb for meaning. Reincarnation, with its corollary concept, the immortality of the soul, is a most fruitful and comforting idea for those who have considered death to be a move into oblivion. Loved ones remain, perhaps to be seen again. Earth, with its glories, its interwoven cycles, its biological and existential mysteries—perhaps we'll see it all again. And life itself—about which so many joke that it is wasted on the young—perhaps we could live it again and with more experience and wisdom. Relationships are never perfect. In fact, people who think they're involved in perfect relationships are inevitably in for a rude shock. So, when a loved one dies there is always room for regret. In this regard, the idea that we might meet again if we need to can assuage some of the guilt that haunts a loving mourner.

We the living, like the newly deceased in the Waiting Place, may well feel resistant to our fate. We've discussed angry ghosts, reluctant ghosts, and ghosts too frustrated with their mourners' behavior to even think of continuing their journey. Perhaps as we await our possible transformation into spirits, we can take comfort and confidence from the possibility that we may not be powerless for very long and that we may pass through great possibilities on our way back to life. From the very start of the journey, those with the faith that they will return can benefit from this perspective: There will be other chances, other lives, other opportunities to advance and eventually to merge with a greater reality.

CHAPTER 7

✌

Conclusion: On Hope

Our shelves hold many books now on the place of faith in science and psychiatry, and on the vicissitudes of man's efforts to love and to be loved. But when it comes to hope, our shelves are bare. The journals are silent. The Encyclopedia Britannica *devotes many columns to the topic of love, and many more to faith. But hope, poor little hope! She is not even listed.*

—Karl Menninger, 1987

Having finished our journey through the four stages of the afterdeath and their possible meaning for our lives, it takes just one more step to complete the circle begun in chapter 1. We re-meet James and Henry, but not to witness their deaths. Instead, I want to expand a little on the kinds of lives they led.

Henry, whose death was relatively gentle, was a buoyant, light-hearted person and a hilarious man. In fact, he had always entertained the fantasy of being a stand-up comedian. As his eclectic approach to a self-created belief system attested, Henry was open to all kinds of ideas, all kinds of people, and a wide range of possibilities.

Henry based his life on possibilities, sometimes slim possibilities. He was a seminar leader, a line of work distinguished by its complete lack of financial security. He began each year with an empty calendar; to keep going, he had to believe that people would be interested in what he had to say and would sign up and pay him for the pleasure of hearing it. Like all self-employed people, it was up to him to generate his entire livelihood, and to do that he had to consider it possible to do so.

James couldn't have been more different. Whereas Henry lived by his open heart, James led with his mind. James was *smart*. He was clever, he was skeptical, he studied the past and took its lessons as empirical data. He was a man closed to the outside chance and fixed on formula: If you did this and this, that and that should happen. And it would. By this method, James had propelled himself into the mainstream of big-city politics and had gained enough power to make a huge difference on his urban scene. But he hadn't done it with optimism; he'd done it by figuring out how things worked.

James could not look at death, especially his own death. Not only did he turn his head away when one of the many who cared for him tried to mention it, even his eyes strained away, like those of a terrified horse attempting to avoid the sight of a fire.

There were many differences between these two friends of mine, but there was a crux to the differences, a point from which all the rest stemmed. Once I saw it I wondered how I could have missed it before. The crux of the differences was this: All his life, Henry had *hope*; James, never.

What precisely is hope? It is not as easy a word to understand as we might think, using it as we do so often and in so many ways. We often include it in the most mundane of all expressions: Hope all is well! Hope you do okay! Hope to see you soon! On the surface, hope is not a word that carries much weight or momentum. Yet it is hope that slays the rational mind and enables us to expand beyond normal human boundaries.

Menninger's dismay at the lack of literature on hope, expressed in the epigraph to this chapter, still largely holds true.[1] Jung, in the two meager citations to the subject in his collected works, poetically calls hope one of the four highest "human endeavors . . . or graces,"—the other three being understanding, love, and faith.[2] C. S. Snyder, whose research on hope has been the most extensive, gives us a scientific definition of hope, breaking the quality into two components: a pathway perceived toward one or more goals and the capacity to move down that pathway.[3] Psychologist E. Stotland defines hope as "an expectation greater than zero of achieving a goal."[4]

A few years ago, a definition of *physical suffering* that came to me by word of mouth made reference to the significance of hope. *Suffering,* went this definition, is "chronic pain minus hope." With the desire and expectation that pain will diminish, most people can tolerate any level of physical pain. It's only when hope disappears that patients come to believe that their pain will never go away—that enduring distress becomes true suffering.

Without hope, we human beings suffer. With hope, anything we imagine might be possible.

Maurice Lamm, in *The Power of Hope,* says it well: "Whether we admit it or not, many of us are afraid to hope—and we are afraid *of* hope as well. Maybe we equate it with taking a chance, with the long shot, with reckless gambling on the future. Risk-taking may be so contrary to the Puritan ethic by which we are raised that we are embarrassed even to admit to anyone that what we have to depend upon in the conduct of our life is hope—as if it were some will-o'-the-wisp and more sensible people would give short shrift to it. The fact is, hope is none of these. Hope *is* our future. It is our big chance. It is where our true love lies."[5]

Another writer, contemporary philosopher Sam Keen, tells a poignant story of the upwelling of hope in his life:

In the months immediately following my father's death in 1964, my grief was intensified by intellectual agony as I struggled to find reasons to believe in some deathless and kindly power who might be called God. At the time I was still teaching the philosophy of religion at Louisville, so there was an additional pressure from my colleagues to produce a statement of faith that would be acceptable to the congregation of believers who paid our salaries. But the more I tried to storm the heavens, the more disturbed I became. I could find no answers.

One morning as I walked to work through a park, in the middle of a large field the sky seemed to open. A voice from the infinite silence within and beyond me said: "You don't have to know." I was flooded with an immense sense of relief, as if a thousand-pound weight had been lifted from my shoulders. Perhaps for the first time in my life, I was free from the compulsion to discover an explanation for my existence. My mind relaxed in the knowledge that I could never have certain knowledge of the ultimate context of my existence.

In the presence of death, my mind had reached its limit and found new freedom. Disillusioned, I discovered hope. Hope, as opposed to illusion or optimism, is not predicated on things to come. Nor is it a claim to possess some special knowledge or revelation of a hidden future, in which all evil is redeemed and all death negated. To hope we must know that we can not know the limits of the Ever-Creating Power that has, is, and will bring all that is into being. And beyond that, we must trust that the inexhaustible mystery we touch when we discover our soul-spirit-freedom-capacity-to-transcend provides our best clue to the nature of Being. . . . Hope begins with the realization that human experience is finally inadequate to deal with all the possibilities reality harbors.[6]

My friend James put all his faith in human experience and expected no break from the universe. He assessed, analyzed, planned, and created backup options as he went along—he had no hope that the anxieties of life would be resolved, and he lived his life accordingly. As for death, James allowed no possibility that its awfulness might be mitigated by realities he could not know. Though James, like Henry, was a funny man—his humor was rooted in his skeptical and hard-boiled view of the world. He suffered from the lack of expectation that things could be other than they seemed.

All the way through the arc of existence, from the beginning of childhood through the transit into the afterdeath, hope is what makes the difference. With it, we admit all possibilities. Without it, pain or suffering can hold dominion.

The human spirit is fired from within by both an irrepressible curiosity about the future and an urge to improve the present. Even people who have been traumatized and defeated—those subjected to the unrelenting degradation of death camps, those raped and tortured in war—

even most of them, when it is safe, step outside and squint at the sky and eventually return to life. In the general scheme of things human, hope is irrepressible and unexpungeable. In fact, although we have been told that Pandora withheld this quality of being from us, it isn't possible. Hope is inherent in the human experience.

Hope is nothing less than the fullest expression of life itself—life without borders, life after death, the infinite possibilities open to us as we prepare to journey beyond the existence we know. Like any travelers, we yearn for smooth passage for ourselves and each other and ardently wish each other well. We prepare as best we can for a destination whose name we cannot know—and whose true nature, from this side of death, we can only imagine.

APPENDICES

ॐ

The Afterdeath Inventory

In 1988, I came to believe that an exploration of the afterdeath could somehow contribute to my efforts to assist my clients in experiencing gentle deaths; I turned to the community of thinkers and writers whom I knew would have an interest in the subject and asked them directly, "Do you think a cross-cultural exploration of afterdeath beliefs, with the eventual goal of bringing these ideas into the culture, is a good idea?" Each of the twenty-some experts in death and dying and others from related fields answered "yes" and then elaborated from his or her particular point of view. It took me about a year to gather and integrate their thoughts. One of the people I spoke with during this process stood out from the others in what I learned from our meeting.

She was a psychiatrist who specialized in terminally ill clients and whose work I respected very much. I flew to Washington to meet with her; we had a delightful dinner together, and over coffee I asked her, not my formal questions, but one that I had very much wanted to ask of her. "Tell me, what are your clients' most common responses to questions about the afterdeath? What do they tell you about what they think will happen to them when they die?"

Long silence. Much looking around. Finally, she answered, "Sukie, I've got to tell you. I've never succeeded in bringing it up."

I hope my eyes didn't widen too noticeably.

"I'm always on the verge of asking about it," she continued, "but I just can't find the words. I'm very unsure of the questions to ask on this particular subject." Again, she looked away and repeated, "I just can't find the words."

I was amazed. I had been sure that dialogues on the afterdeath were becoming commonplace, at least as a part of counseling and psychiatry. I flew home to New York and over a long weekend wrote the first draft of the Afterdeath Inventory. The purpose was to fill the void to which my dinner companion had alluded: to provide the words, the questions, that would initiate a dialogue on a topic that few people entered into on their own—and that even professionals may avoid. An overall goal of the inventory was to elicit a person's underlying beliefs and concerns about the afterdeath.

It was quite a challenge. The inventory had to draw not only from those ideas that might be familiar to those who would take it but also from ideas and beliefs of the peoples I was studying around the world. I divided the possible ways of thinking about the afterdeath into seven separate panels of questions, asking the respondent to provide these categories of information:

- their general views on the afterdeath;
- their personal identity there in the afterdeath;
- the environment in their afterdeath;
- how they could prepare for the afterdeath;
- influences on the afterdeath;
- their future in the afterdeath;
- and their evidence for the existence and nature of the afterdeath.

Every item on the Inventory had its origin in at least one cultural system or religion of the world. I advised a way to turn the responses on the Inventory into the beginning of a dialogue and described ways of using the Inventory within various contexts.

Then I revised and revised and revised.

The resulting seven-panel series of questions is meant to be taken by a range of people attempting to come to terms with the afterdeath. These are possible benefits:

- The effort can bring clarity to an area of our being that is otherwise vague.
- That clarity in turn can help us prepare more fully to face our own deaths and those of others.
- Consciously evoking and affirming our understanding of the afterdeath brings comfort and allays fear in the face of our own deaths, the deaths of others, the "minideaths" and losses that occur all throughout life.
- Answering questions and writing statements about the afterdeath can help us articulate our personal beliefs.

People in the process of dying are the most obvious candidates for benefiting from answering questions on the afterdeath. But, as my psychiatrist friend made clear, the wide variety of professionals who assist in the dying process—health care workers, clergy, psychologists, and other kinds of counselors—can benefit, too, not only from asking but from answering such questions. The same is true of family and friends—loved ones who stand to the side, often uncertain about what to do as a person they care about passes from life into the afterdeath.

For all these people, the Afterdeath Inventory provides a way of organizing and focusing information that is very hard to think or talk about. Shrouded in diverse traditions, often learned in childhood and later rejected, answers and intuitions about that "someplace else" tease and elude us as does nothing else in our lives. Universally, fears and hesitancies swirl around death. In the context of the Inventory, insights and intuitions, however vague, can begin to find articulate expression, and fears of the unknown can come into awareness where they can be confronted and discussed openly.

Each panel has two parts—a multiple-choice questionnaire and a page for writing "caring statements" based on your multiple-choice responses and beginning with the word *I*. I settled on the word *care*— rather than *believe,* for example—in order to evoke resonances or intuitions as well as fully formed insights or beliefs.

The Inventory isn't a test; there are no right or wrong answers. In fact, there are no answers at all, just possibilities. In contemplating statements, open not only your mind but your imagination to them as well. After all, we're reflecting on what reality beyond death *might* consist of, not on empirical facts that can be tested and retested scientifically. The very images and ideas that float up from within you may be custom-designed to ease concerns and worries that have long disturbed you regarding your death, losses in your life, or the deaths of people you love.

Note also that you may take the whole inventory in one sitting or choose only those parts that interest you. Finish quickly, in an hour, or answer questions intermittently, over the course of a month. Again, there is no right or wrong way of using each panel. Adapt your style of responding to your particular interests.

You'll find that the Inventory is redundant; it asks you to return to the questions in each panel twice. The reasoning behind this is to allow you to consider the beliefs you hold while permitting new ones to emerge.

Here's a guide in filling in the Inventory:

Part A: In the circle following each question (Part A), place a check if the sentence makes sense to you.

Part B: Following each question, rank your level of caring (either positively or negatively) by circling a number using these criteria:

- Circle 1 if you care *little* about the statement.
- Circle 2 if you care *somewhat* about the statement.
- Circle 3 if you care *considerably.*
- Circle 4 if you care *a lot.*

Part C: In this part you will actually express yourself in your own words. On the lined page following the questionnaire, write full sentences about the aspect of the afterdeath covered by the particular panel you are working on.

- For those statements where you circled a 2, complete the sentence beginning with the words "I care somewhat that _____."

- For those question where you circled a 3, complete the sentence beginning with the words "I care considerably that
  _____."
- For those sentences where you circled a 4, complete the sentence beginning with the words "I care a lot that
  _____."

While you are taking the Inventory, if other statements occur to you that reflect your beliefs—and this happens frequently—add them to Part C along with your responses.

When you complete Part C, the result will be a record of your current thinking on the afterdeath. By reflecting on Part C, you will see in black and white what you carry within you, and you will have a language and a starting place for discussing those ideas and images, even if the discussion is an internal monologue held only with yourself. You may already have given deep and focused thought to the issues identified on the Inventory. In this case, with these concerns clearly on paper, you'll be able to return to them again and again— perhaps only briefly, perhaps with sustained thought. The Inventory is designed not only to permit dialogue and thus reduce isolation, but to also allay anxieties and bring comfort to areas within and below awareness.

Section I

My General View on the Afterdeath

		Part A	Part B
I-1	I will probably be in a static state in the afterdeath	O	1 2 3 4
I-2	I will probably go on a journey of some kind in the afterdeath.	O	1 2 3 4
I-3	The afterdeath will probably take a stipulated amount of time.	O	1 2 3 4
I-4	The afterdeath will probably have a goal.	O	1 2 3 4

		Part A	Part B
I-5	The afterdeath will probably be personally transformational.	O	1 2 3 4
I-6	I will probably benefit from my afterdeath experiences.	O	1 2 3 4
I-7	Those I have loved will probably benefit from my afterdeath experiences.	O	1 2 3 4
I-8	My community will probably benefit from my afterdeath experiences.	O	1 2 3 4
I-9	Humanity as a whole will probably benefit from my afterdeath experiences.	O	1 2 3 4
I-10	The goal of the afterdeath will be to return to life.	O	1 2 3 4
I-11	The goal of the afterdeath will be to go to another form of life.	O	1 2 3 4
I-12	The goal of the afterdeath will be to rest.	O	1 2 3 4
I-13	The goal of the afterdeath will be to achieve eternal bliss.	O	1 2 3 4
I-14	The goal of the afterdeath will be to become one with all beings.	O	1 2 3 4
I-15	There will be a resting place or waiting place that begins the afterdeath.	O	1 2 3 4
I-16	The afterdeath is probably random.	O	1 2 3 4
I-17	The afterdeath is probably a condition.	O	1 2 3 4
I-18	The afterdeath is probably a place.	O	1 2 3 4
I-19	I will probably review my life in the afterdeath.	O	1 2 3 4
I-20	I will probably experience light in the afterdeath.	O	1 2 3 4
I-21	I will probably experience darkness in the afterdeath.	O	1 2 3 4
I-22	I will probably experience pleasure in the afterdeath.	O	1 2 3 4
I-23	I will probably experience pain in the afterdeath.	O	1 2 3 4
I-24	I will probably experience peace in the afterdeath.	O	1 2 3 4

		Part A	Part B
I-25	I will probably experience terror in the afterdeath.	O	1 2 3 4
I-26	I will probably experience bliss in the afterdeath.	O	1 2 3 4
I-27	I will not be judged in the afterdeath.	O	1 2 3 4
I-28	I will probably learn important lessons in the afterdeath.	O	1 2 3 4
I-29	I will probably experience tests in the afterdeath.	O	1 2 3 4
I-30	I will probably experience suffering in the afterdeath.	O	1 2 3 4
I-31	I will probably experience condemnation in the afterdeath.	O	1 2 3 4
I-32	I will probably experience judgment in the afterdeath.	O	1 2 3 4
I-33	I will be judged by the tally system in the afterdeath.	O	1 2 3 4
I-34	I will be judged by the karma system in the afterdeath.	O	1 2 3 4
I-35	I will be judged by the challenge system in the afterdeath.	O	1 2 3 4
I-36	I will be judged by myself in the afterdeath.	O	1 2 3 4
I-37	I will be judged through an experiential life review in the afterdeath.	O	1 2 3 4
I-38	There will probably be a guide to help me in the afterdeath.		
I-39	I will probably have insights in the afterdeath.	O	1 2 3 4
I-40	_____	O	1 2 3 4
I-41	_____	O	1 2 3 4

My General Views on the Afterdeath (Part C)

Having completed Parts A and B at your leisure, please list those statements about which you care somewhat (2), care considerably (3), and care a lot (4). Please write full sentences beginning *(4) I care a lot*

that _____ *or (3) I care considerably that* _____ *or*
(2) I care somewhat that _____.

_____

_____

_____

_____

_____

_____

_____

_____

_____

_____

_____

_____

_____

_____

_____

_____

_____

_____

Section II

Who I Might Be in the Afterdeath

		Part A	Part B
II-1	I will be pure consciousness in the afterdeath.	○	1 2 3 4
II-2	I will be pure energy in the afterdeath.	○	1 2 3 4
II-3	I will have a form in the afterdeath.	○	1 2 3 4
II-4	I will be formless in the afterdeath.	○	1 2 3 4
II-5	I will be able to communicate with the living from the afterdeath.	○	1 2 3 4

		Part A	Part B
II-6	I will be able to communicate with my former community from the afterdeath.	O	1 2 3 4
II-7	I will be able to communicate with those living that I love from the afterdeath.	O	1 2 3 4
II-8	I will bring aspects of my body with me to the afterdeath.	O	1 2 3 4
II-9	I will bring aspects of my life history to the afterdeath.	O	1 2 3 4
II-10	I will bring problems that I have not resolved in this life with me into the afterdeath.	O	1 2 3 4
II-11	I will stay the same in the afterdeath.	O	1 2 3 4
II-12	I will have been anticipated in the afterdeath.	O	1 2 3 4
II-13	I will have memory in the afterdeath.	O	1 2 3 4
II-14	I will have a sense of humor in the afterdeath.	O	1 2 3 4
II-15	I will be masculine in the afterdeath.	O	1 2 3 4
II-16	I will be feminine in the afterdeath.	O	1 2 3 4
II-17	I will be without gender in the afterdeath.	O	1 2 3 4
II-18	I will perceive only (not judge) in the afterdeath.	O	1 2 3 4
II-19	I will be able to move about in the afterdeath.	O	1 2 3 4
II-20	I will be able to see in the afterdeath.	O	1 2 3 4
II-21	I will be able to hear in the afterdeath.	O	1 2 3 4
II-22	I will be able to touch in the afterdeath.	O	1 2 3 4
II-23	I will be able to eat in the afterdeath.	O	1 2 3 4
II-24	I will be able to smell in the afterdeath.	O	1 2 3 4
II-25	I will have energy in the afterdeath.	O	1 2 3 4
II-26	I will have volition in the afterdeath.	O	1 2 3 4
II-27	I will be passive in the afterdeath.	O	1 2 3 4
II-28	I will perceive beauty in the afterdeath.	O	1 2 3 4
II-29	I will perceive ugliness in the afterdeath.	O	1 2 3 4
II-30	I will experience love in the afterdeath.	O	1 2 3 4
II-31	I will experience hate in the afterdeath.	O	1 2 3 4

		Part A	Part B
II-32	I will experience creativity in the afterdeath.	○	1 2 3 4
II-33	I will experience inertia in the afterdeath.	○	1 2 3 4
II-34	I will experience ecstasy in the afterdeath.	○	1 2 3 4
II-35	I will experience despair in the afterdeath.	○	1 2 3 4
II-36	I will experience happiness in the afterdeath.	○	1 2 3 4
II-37	I will experience sadness in the afterdeath.	○	1 2 3 4
II-38	I will experience rage in the afterdeath.	○	1 2 3 4
II-39	I will experience comfort in the afterdeath.	○	1 2 3 4
II-40	I will experience pride in the afterdeath.	○	1 2 3 4
II-41	I will experience humility in the afterdeath.	○	1 2 3 4
II-42	I will experience sexual energy in the afterdeath.	○	1 2 3 4
II-43	I will travel alone in the afterdeath.	○	1 2 3 4
II-44	I will travel in groups in the afterdeath.	○	1 2 3 4
II-45	There will be other travelers in the afterdeath.	○	1 2 3 4
II-46	The other travelers will be divided into groups or types in the afterdeath.	○	1 2 3 4
II-47	I will attend some kind of school in the afterdeath.	○	1 2 3 4
II-48	I will have a teacher in the afterdeath.	○	1 2 3 4
II-49	I will evolve into a higher being in the afterdeath.	○	1 2 3 4
II-50	_____	○	1 2 3 4
II-51	_____		

Who I Might Be in the Afterdeath (Part C)

Having completed Parts A and B at your leisure, please list those statements about which you care somewhat (2), care considerably (3), and care a lot (4). Please write full sentences beginning *(4) I care a lot that* _____ or *(3) I care considerably that* _____ or *(2) I care somewhat that* _____.

_____
_____
_____
_____
_____
_____
_____
_____
_____
_____
_____
_____
_____
_____
_____
_____
_____
_____
_____
_____

SECTION III

How I Might Prepare for the Afterdeath

		Part A	Part B
IV-1	I can prepare throughout my entire life for the afterdeath.	◯	1 2 3 4
IV-2	I can prepare only at specific times in my life for the afterdeath.	◯	1 2 3 4
IV-3	I can prepare in specific aspects of my life for the afterdeath.	◯	1 2 3 4
IV-4	I can prepare through my relationships to others for the afterdeath.	◯	1 2 3 4
IV-5	I can prepare through my work for the afterdeath.	◯	1 2 3 4

		Part A	Part B
IV-6	I can prepare through service for the afterdeath.	O	1 2 3 4
IV-7	I can prepare through action for the afterdeath.	O	1 2 3 4
IV-8	I can prepare through detachment for the afterdeath.	O	1 2 3 4
IV-9	I can prepare through my handling of finances for the afterdeath.	O	1 2 3 4
IV-10	I can prepare through my sexuality for the afterdeath.	O	1 2 3 4
IV-11	I can prepare through charity for the afterdeath.	O	1 2 3 4
IV-12	I can prepare through my belief system for the afterdeath.	O	1 2 3 4
IV-13	I can prepare through meditation for the afterdeath.	O	1 2 3 4
IV-14	I can prepare through penitence for the afterdeath.	O	1 2 3 4
IV-15	I can prepare through prayer for the afterdeath.	O	1 2 3 4
IV-16	I can prepare through ritual observances for the afterdeath.	O	1 2 3 4
IV-17	I can prepare for the afterdeath by reading.	O	1 2 3 4
IV-18	I can prepare for the afterdeath by providing substantial funds for my funeral.	O	1 2 3 4
IV-19	I can prepare for the afterdeath by gathering objects to bring with me.	O	1 2 3 4
IV-20	I can prepare for the afterdeath by providing another home for my family to move to after I die.	O	1 2 3 4
IV-21	I can prepare for the afterdeath by understanding my past lives.	O	1 2 3 4
IV-22	I can prepare for the afterdeath through the taking of (sacred) drug substances.	O	1 2 3 4
IV-23	I can prepare for the afterdeath by resolving problematic relationships.	O	1 2 3 4

	Part A	Part B
IV-24 I can prepare for the afterdeath by a life of harmlessness.	○	1 2 3 4
IV-25 I can prepare for the afterdeath by a life of piety.	○	1 2 3 4
IV-26 _____	○	1 2 3 4
IV-27 _____	○	

How I Might Prepare for the Afterdeath (Part C)

Having completed Parts A and B at your leisure, please list those statements about which you care somewhat (2), care considerably (3), and care a lot (4). Please write full sentences beginning *(4) I care a lot that* _____ or *(3) I care considerably that* _____ or *(2) I care somewhat that* _____.

Section IV

How I Believe the Nature of My Afterdeath Is Determined

		Part A	Part B
V-1	The nature of my afterdeath is affected by the life I have lived.	O	1 2 3 4
V-2	The nature of my afterdeath is affected by the moment of my death.	O	1 2 3 4
V-3	The nature of my afterdeath is affected by rituals performed at the time of my death.	O	1 2 3 4
V-4	The nature of my afterdeath is affected by rituals performed for me at intervals after my death.	O	1 2 3 4
V-5	The nature of my afterdeath is affected by the actual time of my death.	O	1 2 3 4
V-6	The nature of my afterdeath is affected by the cause of my death.	O	1 2 3 4
V-7	The nature of my afterdeath is affected by my psychological state at the time of my death.	O	1 2 3 4
V-8	The nature of my afterdeath is affected by the attitudes of my friends at the time of my death.	O	1 2 3 4
V-9	The nature of my afterdeath is affected by the attitudes of my family at the time of my death.	O	1 2 3 4
V-10	The nature of my afterdeath is affected by the manner in which I am buried.	O	1 2 3 4
V-11	The nature of my afterdeath is determined before my birth (i.e., predestined).	O	1 2 3 4
V-12	By merely having considered aspects of the afterdeath, I prepare for it.	O	1 2 3 4
V-13	_____	O	1 2 3 4
V-14	_____	O	1 2 3 4

How I Believe the Nature of the Afterdeath Is Determined (Part C)

Having completed Parts A and B at your leisure, please list those statements about which you care somewhat (2), care considerably (3), and care a lot (4). Please write full sentences beginning *(4) I care a lot that* _____ or *(3) I care considerably that* _____ or *(2) I care somewhat that* _____.

Section V

What I Think Happens to Me *AFTER* the Afterdeath

		Part A	*Part B*
VI-1	What happens to me after the afterdeath is determined during the afterdeath.	O	1 2 3 4
VI-2	What happens to me after the afterdeath is determined by random selection.	O	1 2 3 4
VI-3	What happens to me after the afterdeath is determined by the nature of my journey.	O	1 2 3 4
VI-4	What happens to me after the afterdeath is determined by my accumulated lives.	O	1 2 3 4
VI-5	What happens to me after the afterdeath is determined by my willful intent.	O	1 2 3 4
VI-6	What happens to me after the afterdeath is determined by someone or something else.	O	1 2 3 4
VI-7	There will probably be a specific time for my return and it will be decided before the afterdeath.	O	1 2 3 4

I Think the Following Will Probably Be Determined in the Afterdeath

VI-8	My mother.	O	1 2 3 4
VI-9	My father.	O	1 2 3 4
VI-10	My birth order in the family.	O	1 2 3 4
VI-11	My sex.	O	1 2 3 4
VI-12	My country.	O	1 2 3 4
VI-13	My DNA structure.	O	1 2 3 4
VI-14	I will become energy only in the afterdeath.	O	1 2 3 4
VI-15	I will not return to this life from the afterdeath.	O	1 2 3 4
VI-16	_____	O	1 2 3 4
VI-17	_____	O	1 2 3 4

What I Think Happens to Me *AFTER* the Afterdeath (Part C)

Having completed Parts A and B at your leisure, please list those statements about which you care somewhat (2), care considerably (3), and care a lot (4). Please write full sentences beginning *(4) I care a lot that* _____ or *(3) I care considerably that* _____ or *(2) I care somewhat that* _____.

Section VI

My Personal Evidence

		Part A	Part B
VII-1	My personal evidence about the afterdeath is formed, in part, by visual experiences I have had.	○	1 2 3 4
VII-2	My personal evidence about the afterdeath is formed, in part, by technically mediated experiences I have had.	○	1 2 3 4
VII-3	My personal evidence about the afterdeath is formed, in part, by tactile experiences I have had.	○	1 2 3 4
VII-4	My personal evidence about the afterdeath is formed, in part, by auditory experiences I have had.	○	1 2 3 4
VII-5	My personal evidence about the afterdeath is formed, in part, by olfactory experiences I have had.	○	1 2 3 4
VII-6	My personal evidence about the afterdeath is formed, in part, by taste experiences I have had.	○	1 2 3 4
VII-7	My personal evidence about the afterdeath is formed, in part, by everyday experiences I have had.	○	1 2 3 4
VII-8	My personal evidence about the afterdeath is formed, in part, by humanly mediated experiences I have had (e.g., with psychics, clairvoyants, channelers, mediums, et al.).	○	1 2 3 4
VII-9	My personal evidence about the afterdeath is formed, in part, by predicted experiences I have had, e.g., arrangements made before someone close died for a signal from them after that person's death.	○	1 2 3 4

		Part A	Part B
VII-10	My personal evidence about the afterdeath is formed, in part, by what I have read.	○	1 2 3 4
VII-11	My personal evidence about the afterdeath is formed, in part, by stories I have heard.	○	1 2 3 4
VII-13	My personal evidence about the afterdeath is formed, in part, by experiences of internal bodily states that I have had.	○	1 2 3 4
VII-14	My personal evidence about the afterdeath is formed, in part, by my religious training.	○	1 2 3 4
VII-15	My personal evidence about the afterdeath is formed, in part, by experiences I have had with ghosts, beings, or forces.	○	1 2 3 4
VII-16	My personal evidence about the afterdeath is formed, in part, through prayer.	○	1 2 3 4
VII-17	My personal evidence about the afterdeath is formed, in part, through meditation.	○	1 2 3 4
VII-18	My personal evidence about the afterdeath is formed, in part, by my vital imagination.	○	1 2 3 4
VII-19	My personal evidence about the afterdeath has come from family members.	○	1 2 3 4
VII-20	_____	○	1 2 3 4
VII-21	_____		

My Personal Evidence for My Beliefs (Part C)

Having completed Parts A and B at your leisure, please list those statements about which you care somewhat (2), care considerably (3), and care a lot (4). Please write full sentences beginning *(4) I care a lot that* _____ or *(3) I care considerably that* _____ or *(2) I care somewhat that* _____.

_____

_____

_____

_____

_____

_____

⚙

The Senior Researchers:

Institute for the Study of the Afterdeath

The Institute for the Study of the Afterdeath has engaged many people around the world to gather data. These colleagues, called senior researchers, lived in the countries of the groups we were studying and were familiar with these particular peoples. Frequently it was they who suggested tribes or cults rich in afterdeath beliefs. It would have been foolish to assume that members of most of these groups would have spoken freely with foreigners posing "silly" questions, much less that they would willingly meet with us in their sacred spaces. Finding people to serve as senior researchers was thus a major task of the Institute. It usually took a year to make a selection, the criteria starting with the requirement that candidates have free access to the group in question and that they speak English. No data-gathering trip could go forward without the selection of senior researchers.

All senior researchers had full access to the groups upon whom they reported, and all were trusted and welcomed by the elders of the people. Some had been born into the group and had left to seek a formal education. Others were academics who had devoted their careers to studying groups we wished to learn from. And some were curators who, through their collection and preservation of a group's art, were known and trusted. One senior researcher was a cartographer, two were emeritus professors, another was finishing his doctorate. One was a mask-maker/priest, and the remaining senior researchers were professors of the humanities. It was this wonderful mix of people who, in country after country, introduced us to the "tradition bearers," or keepers of the indigenous group's wisdom, and made sure we did not inadvertently offend. They conducted our research on the afterdeath not with the man on the street of particular groups but with the selected shamans, priests, holy people, healers, and psychics who were *leaders*. In our time in the country, Edmundo and I met with the majority of those to be interviewed. After we left, the senior researchers spent the following year formally conducting the research we required on our standardized research instrument of 180 questions.

Senior researchers often used up to twenty hours and made repeated visits just to complete the questionnaire with one of the five selected representatives of a group. In many cases, the researchers found not only that they had to return repeatedly to gather the data, but that they had to *translate* onto paper the whole of the research instrument before they could even begin to gather any data whatsoever.

Of this dedicated group, special thanks must go to Portuguese psychologist Mariana Caudida Caixeoro, who introduced us to the Mahapatra in Varanasi, India, for her flexibility and superior work; to cartographer Max Knaus-Rojas and his wife Lily Knaus-Rojas, who worked with the Torajas of Sulawesi, Indonesia, trekking and traveling to find old, wonderful tradition bearers who remembered; to generous and gracious Professor Alagoa and his son, David, who took us "home" to Nembe, up the Niger Delta, past the wonder of the stork nests; to two generations of Krishnas, of Varanasi, who entertained and escorted Edmundo and me through some of our more amusing and thought provoking adventures; to Aditya Behl and his whole family who, aside from all else, introduced us to a simply unforgettable lamb dinner.

I also wish to thank Bade Ajuwon and his assistant for their good humor—their look of shock and then adroit translations when I insisted that a goat being sacrificed to heal me from a slight illness be neither a female nor a youngster. To Dr. Amelie Degbelo Iroko who, aside from completing the entire Benin research single-handedly, graciously accompanied me as we dropped all pressures of research to "hit" the market, I am truly grateful; likewise, Edmundo wishes me to be sure to thank Ernest Emenyonu for his life-saving tip on where to get hamburgers and French fries in Lagos. Ken Ring generously supported and assisted on the Near-Death Experiences, from the very beginning, via rapid phone, fax, and E-mail; I Made and Judy attended wonderfully to all needs in Bali; and Julio Braga searched for well over an hour on a cracked telephone line between Sao Paulo, Brazil; Bahia, Brazil; and New York City until we came upon the word *traveler* as an acceptable cross-cultural word for the spirit. Bob and Elaine Schroder and their family of Juneau, Alaska, were wonderful, on-the-spot hosts, and Dr. Hernando Guimaraes Andrade of Brazil was available in such a plethora of ways that it is impossible to mention them all here. Juanito de Santos opened many doors for us, and thanks go, too, to Dr. Bezerra De Menezes, who graciously allowed his students of Campus Universitario to work with us; to the Centro de Trabalho Indigenista, who made sense of the most complex information on the Brazilian Indians; and to Ade Grassa, who judiciously and wisely gave us access and information while simultaneously protecting the revered Egun. To all, thank you for your work and the wealth of enduring personal memories.

The following is a list of the senior researchers and their brief descriptions of the tribes or groups from which they selected the tradition bearers and interviewed them.

AFRICA

The Yoruba

The Yoruba belief system of Nigeria is based on belief in and relationship with numerous deities. Called *Orisas,* the deities are said to number 401, but this figure is meant as a poetic one, to convey the many gods, and not as a numerical accounting. The Yoruba believe that it is by means of their combination of human and spiritual qualities that the gods understand human problems and will address them promptly when necessary rituals are offered.

In association with the Yoruba medicine men and shamans:

A.U. Iware, Ph.D., Former Acting Director
Institute of African Studies
University of Ibadan
Ibadan, Nigeria

The Yoruba medicine men and shamans are dedicated to the god *Ifa*, perhaps the most important of all the gods. Ifa built his immense wisdom into a system of divination through which humans could talk with him as well as the other gods. The literary texts that Ifa priests chant during the process of divination represent a system that has preserved their culture, philosophy, mythology, and folk medicine. Ifa is consulted in practically every aspect of human life, including naming, illness, death, marriage.

In association with the Yoruba hunters:

Bade Ajuwon, Ph.D., Director
Institute of Cultural Studies
Obafemi Awolowo University
Ile-Ife, Nigeria

The Yoruba Hunter Guild is dedicated to *Ogun*, the god of iron, welfare, and heroism, who supervises and regulates the hunting occupation—one of the oldest professions of humankind. Ogun is seen as a war leader and is very important among the other gods because of the protection he gives.

The Fon People of Benin

In association with the Fon voodoo practitioners and Wemenu and Ouidah Fon healers and diviners:

Amelie Degbelo Spouse Iroko, Ph.D.
Beninian Center for Scientific and Technical Research
Contounu, Republic of Benin, West Africa

The Fon healers, diviners, and voodoo practitioners: The Fon are numerically the most significant ethnic group of the Benin Republic of Africa. From the sixteenth to the nineteenth centuries the Fon developed a military state called Danxome, famous over West Africa and Europe for its female soldiers, known as "the amazon" warriors. This kingdom took part in the transatlantic slave trade, which led to the dissemination of its culture in many parts of the American and Brazilian continents, thereby originating the voodoo cult in Haiti and strongly influencing the Candomble religion of Brazil.

The Igbo of Nigeria

In association with the Igbo healers, diviners, and experts:

Ernest N. Emenyonu, Ph.D.
Provost and Chief Executive
Alvan Ikoku College of Education
Owerri, Imo State
Nigeria

The Igbo diviners, healers, and experts of South Western Nigeria conceive of their Ancestors as members of their current families. The Ancestors are scolded as if they were still living, fed as if they were hungry, and reprimanded for failing their duties to the family by causing premature deaths, crop failures, and unprofitable trade. The Igbo belief that the Ancestors come back to "social" life is rooted in their theory of reincarnation and transmigration.

The Ijo of Nigeria

In association with the traditional Ijo diviners and Christian Ijo of Nembe:

Professor Emeritus E. J. Alagoa
History Department
Faculty of the Humanities
University of Port Harcourt
Port Harcourt, Nigeria

The Ijo cult is of the Nembe region of the Niger Delta of Nigeria. The early European visitors, particularly the British, referred to the Nembe as the Brass people, a name that appears on many colonial maps, books, and documents. Their traditional religion relates to the worship of water spirits and the veneration of the Ancestors. The totems of the Ijo are the royal python and the African python, both of which represent the national god Ogidiga. All gods of the Ijo communities in the Niger Delta area are subordinate to Ogidiga and are represented in terms of kinship—i.e., as his children, wives, and so on.

Christianity was introduced to the Ijo in the late 1800s, and most Ijo have converted and commingled their early beliefs with a Christian view of the afterdeath.

Ijo priests and priestesses of cults dedicated to linking the living to the dead, called diviners, do still exist.

BRAZIL

(under the general direction of Edmundo Barbosa)

In association with the Indian Communities of the Guarani and Kadiweu:

Maria Ines Martins Ladeira
and Jaime Garcia Siqueira, Jr.
Centro de Trabalho Indigenista
São Paulo, Brazil

The Guarani Indians form their settlements on the coast with the hope of reaching the Land Without Evil—Paradise—that lies beyond the ocean. According to their mythology and cosmology, all homes, all houses for prayers, and all people who pray through ritual chants and dances must face the direction of the sunrise, the way to the Land Without Evil. There is an increasing belief among the tribe that the world is about to be destroyed by fire. Historic and continual encroachment by whites on their territory underlies the intensification of their migratory movements in search of the Land Without Evil where, the Guarani believe, they can achieve immortality of the soul and of their culture on earth.

The Kadiweu Indians, whose current population is 1,070, were historically known as "The Indian Horsemen," owing to their skilled use of horses in battle. Mythical stories emphasize the need for distance between the living and the dead, and an afterdeath is made possible by burying the dead's belongings with them. So identified and dedicated to their horses were the Kadiweu that the horses were customarily buried with them in order to proceed to an Ancestors' afterdeath community essentially similar to the Kadiweu's living community. Names of the living are changed so as to mark a separation from the dead, whose homes are destroyed at their time of death.

In association with the Spiritist and Umbanda religions:

Dr. Bezerra De Menezes
Campus Universitario
Guirchiva, Brazil

The Spiritist beliefs are based primarily on the theory of European Alan Kardec. In contrast with other Brazilian systems, Spiritism in

Brazil is accessible to everyone and is today one of the most wide-spread belief systems in the country. Spiritists conduct schools, clinics, day care centers, and a university in Brazil and have ongoing and deeply held beliefs in spirits, spirit guides, and spirit groups. They frequently communicate with the dead through seances and work extensively on healing through contact and cleansing of the aura.

The Umbanda religion reflects Brazil's diverse cultural and social history, and includes the influences of the African slaves, the Brazilian Indians, the Roman Catholic catechism, Alan Kardec's principles of Spiritism, and Madame Blavatsky's Theosophy. Although Umbanda has no official codification of patterns of belief, cults, or rituals, there is a common practice of good works and charity, a belief in the continuation of life after death, and the ability to communicate with spirits. Practiced in temples and centers throughout Brazil, dance accompanied by folk songs and drumming assists initiates into altered states, at which time the dancers are possessed by the spirits of long-dead Indians and Afro-Brazilian slaves who give counsel on life problems.

In association with Candomble and the Egun community:

Dr. Julio Braga, former Director
Center for Afro-Oriental Studies
University of Bahia
Bahia, Brazil
and
Ade Grassa
Bahia, Brazil

Candomble is an Afro-Brazilian religion that includes a great number of religious elements from the African Fon and Yoruba cultures (historically linked by the slave traffic to Brazil) and Roman Catholicism. Candomble ritual includes rhythmic dances that evoke trance states and the possession of the dancers who are extensively trained initiates. These rituals consist of an invocation of the deities from the

Afro-Brazilian pantheon who, through possession of the initiated, come to socialize, counsel, and give spiritual support to the community of the faithful.

The Cult of the Egun is that aspect of Candomble that is dedicated specifically to the dead and the afterdeath wherein the spirit leaves the body and joins the Ancestors. The Ancestor spirits are known as the Egun, who are also called "the living dead." The Egun cult is a male initiatic cult that has the basic function of invoking the spirits of the Ancestors, who then return to this life to dance during public ceremonies in which they serve as counselors to the religious community.

In general:

Dr. Hernando Guimaraes Andrade
Säo Paulo, Brazil

AMERICA

The Near-Death Experiences:

Professor Emeritus Kenneth Ring
Department of Psychology
University of Connecticut
Storrs, Connecticut

Descriptions of the Near-Death Experience (or NDE) can be found both in literature and historic documents. However, systematic, scientific study of NDEs is a recent undertaking, originating in the mid-1970s. The principal impetus for this work was the publication in 1975 of the *Life after Life* by psychiatrist Raymond A. Moody, Jr. Moody claimed that fifteen "elements" tend to occur with greater or lesser frequency in NDE narratives, thus forming a relatively *constant* NDE pattern. It is estimated that 15 percent of Americans have had NDE experiences.

INDIA

The Mahapatra:

Mariana Caudida Caixeoro
Lisbon, Portugal

The Mahapatra are Brahmin priests who specialize in mortuary rituals. Often less educated than other Brahmin priests and considered untouchable by some, the Mahapatra handle all rituals up to the point where the *preta* (marginal soul) is converted into an Ancestor. Higher castes, believing that meetings with this type of priest bring misfortune and death, often try to avoid facing them.

The Brahmin Hindus, the Sikh Granthis, and the Muslim Sufis who officiate at tombs:

Aditya Behl, Ph.D.
Department of South and Southeast Asian Studies
University of California
Berkeley, California

The Hindu Brahmin represent the complex, polytheistic religion of India. In its earliest days, the Hindu religion focused on the ritual of sacrifice. Later, different classes of sacred literature developed based on mythology and philosophical speculation. Today, orthodox Hindu practice is called *sanatana dharma* and is based on following the stations of life in the caste system, an acceptance of karma and reincarnation, and attendance at temples run by Brahmin priests. The Brahmins interviewed for the Institute of the Study of the Afterdeath are ritual specialists who perform the rites of life and death for the common Hindu.

The Sikh Pandt (path) was founded by Guru Nanak (1469–1539) in Punjab, India, and stresses devotion to the divine Name (Nam), religious teachings in the local vernacular (Punjabi, in this case), the abolition of caste structures, and the guidance of a single guru. Guru Nanak was followed by nine more gurus in succession, who led the community and defined its sense of identity. The most important scripture of the Sikhs is the *Guru Granth Sahib,* a compilation of the writings of the ten gurus and various other medieval saints and poets. After the death of the last guru the book itself became the guru of the Sikh community. Research was conducted with those Sikhs dedicated to this text.

The Muslim Sufis are the descendants of ascetics who tried, in the early days after the death of the Prophet Muhammad, to emulate every action of their prophet in order to get closer to God. The Firdausi Sufis—the group studied for ISA—first came to Bihar, India, in the thirteenth century and soon became the dominant order of this area. The anniversary of the death of the Firdausi Shaikhs is celebrated as marriages with God. Those studied attend the dead.

The Nath People:

Naval Krishna, Ph.D.
Curator
Meharnagarh Museum Trust Fort
Jodhpur, India

The Nath People of India are supposed to be only "spirit," unlike Siva, Vishnu, and Brahma, whom the Nath consider to be intellectuals. The Naths believe in neither the Hindu caste system nor the ashram community, and thus many in subcastes and even many Muslims join this cult. Naths practice a six-fold path of Yoga. Nath Yogis are easily identified at sight by the garland they wear, the hornpipe they carry, an earring, a tiger skin carried on one shoulder to be used as a seat, a bag they carry, a pumpkin pot they carry, a hair knot, the ashes that cover their bodies, their *Selis* (a cotton or wool scarf that yogis and ascetics wind around their heads or necks), and their *khap-pars,* or begging bowls, also carried by yogis and ascetics.

INDONESIA

The Balinese high priests, healers, diviners, keepers of the customs, and priests of the major temple of the dead:

> I Made Surya and Judy Slattum
> Bali, Indonesia/Santa Cruz, California

Agama Hindu Bali, or Hindu Dharma, is the religion of 95 percent of the Balinese. It derives from India via Java and from pre-Hindu animism. In this religion, God is considered to have many manifestations, and the particular manifestation of God one addresses depends on the situation at hand. Prayers for the dead are addressed to God as Betara Siwa, the dissolver and recycler of life. It is the goal of prayer and ceremony in Balinese Hinduism to keep balance in the world, maintaining equilibrium by keeping neither of the two opposites from gaining the upper hand.

The Torajo healers, priests, and others:

> Max Karlheinz Knaus-Rojas, Cartographer
> Sulawesi, Indonesia

The Sa'dan Torajas (pop. 370,000) live approximately 2,500 feet above sea level. The life in animistic Toraja is defined by strict rules called Adat. The creator of mankind—Puang Matua—created 7,777 laws, of which 777 reached the world of mankind. The core of the belief system is the belief in the existence of the soul of people and animals after death and the direct connection of every individual to God through the chain of Ancestors.

✒

The Institute for the Study
of the Afterdeath

The Institute for the Study of the Afterdeath is a nonprofit corporation dedicated to developing worldwide documentation about beliefs and rituals of the afterdeath and using this information to educate the general public and the health care and legal professions. The Institute does not take a position on whether or not an afterdeath actually exists, but rather develops the topic as a field of cross-disciplinary study and encourages and enriches public dialogue on the subject.

The Institute has two main data bases for collecting information concerning the Afterdeath: the Research Grids of Afterdeath Beliefs and BORIAL.

The Research Grids are a series of some one hundred and eighty questions, divided into eight categories that, when completed, allow for statistical as well as discursive analysis. They are administered to representatives of religions, established cults, and other groups worldwide by a team of senior researchers selected in each country. At present, nineteen senior researchers have collaborated to render Grid results on thirty groups in West Africa, Brazil, India, and Indonesia. Among other inquiries, the Grids are analyzed statistically and cross-culturally for common threads and anomalies.

BORIAL (the Brendan O'Reagan Images of the Afterdeath Library) is named after the late vice president of the Institute of Noetic

Sciences, whose idea it was. BORIAL is a computerized system developed and maintained by the Institute that stores, sorts, and prints images depicting the afterdeath by country, religion, symbol, artist, and major color. At present it holds almost five hundred images and is constantly updated.

Public and Professional Education. Information in the data bases lends itself to many forms of presentation, including elementary school curricula, health professions curricula at every level, art books, reference guides, films, and discursive books. The Inventory of Afterdeath Beliefs—a paper-and-pencil packet including a background booklet and eight individual assessment booklets (designated by categories of afterdeath beliefs)—has been developed for use in hospices and by clinicians and the general public. The Research Grids were presented in articles on the Institute in the October 1992 and the October 1995 issues of *OMNI* magazine.

The Institute is supported by private donations and grants.

The Institute for the Study of the Afterdeath was founded and is under the direction of Sukie Miller, Ph.D. Dr. Miller is a former member of the Board of Medical Quality Assurance for the State of California, Director of the Ford Foundation's Confluent Education Project, Director of the Special Education Demonstration Center, Yeshiva Graduate School of Education, member of the Board of the C. G. Jung Institute of San Francisco, Founder and Director of the Institute for the Study of Humanistic Medicine, and a practicing psychotherapist.

APPENDIX D

❧

Recommended Readings
(in a Suggested Order)

Kenneth Krammer, *The Sacred Art of Dying: How World Religions Understand Death* (Paulist Press, 1988).

Farnaz Ma'sumian, *Life after Death: A Study of the Afterdeath of World Religions* (Oxford: Oneworld, 1995).

Kenneth Ring, *Life at Death* (Coward, McCann and Geoghegan, 1980).

Ian Stevenson, M.D., *Children Who Remember Previous Lives* (The University Press of Virginia, 1987).

Aldous Huxley, *The Doors of Perception* (Colophon Books, 1954).

Sogyal Rinpoche, *The Tibetan Book of Living and Dying* (Harper and Collins, 1992).

William James, *The Varieties of Religious Experience* (Penguin, 1982).

Simcha Paull Raphael, *Jewish Views of the Afterlife* (Aronson, 1994).

G. de Puruker, *The Esoteric Traditions*, vol. 1 and 2 (Theosophical University Press, 1973).

Von-Franz, Marie Louise, *On Dreams and Death* (Shambhala, 1984).

NOTES,
BIBLIOGRAPHY,
AND
INDEX

Notes

❧

Only secondary sources cited within the text are documented here. Reference material drawn from data collected in the field are in the Institute for the Study of the Afterdeath archives.

Introduction

1. Sherwin B. Nuland, *How We Die* (New York: Knopf, 1994), p. xvii.

Chapter 1

1. C. J. Jung, *Memories, Dreams, and Reflections* (Vintage Books, 1963), p. 251.
2. Li Po, trans. by Sam Hamill, from Stephen Mitchell, ed., *The Enlightened Heart: An Anthology of Sacred Poetry* (New York: Harper Perennial, 1989), p. 32.

Chapter 2

1. H. Corbin, *Mundus Imaginalis or the Imaginal and the Imagined* (Ipswitch, England, 1972).
2. Kenneth Ring, in Gary Dove, ed., *What Survives?* (Los Angeles: Tarcher, 1990).
3. Michael Talbot, *The Holographic Universe* (New York: Harper Perennial, 1991), pp. 260–61.
4. Fred Allen Wolf, *The Dreaming Universe* (New York: Simon & Schuster, 1995), pp. 260–61.
5. Michael Murphy, *The Transformation of the Body*.

Chapter 3

1. Paul Beard, *Living On* (London: George Allen and Unwin, 1980), p. 90.
2. Annie Besant and C. W. Leadbeater, *Thought Forms* (A Quest Book, 1969), p. 16.
3. Beard, pp. 77–78.
4. Dr. Hernani Guimaraes Andrade, private communication.
5. Frank Gouldsmith Speck, *A Study of the Delaware Indian Big House Ceremony* (Harrisburg, Penn.: Historical Commission, 1931), pp. 174–75.
6. Speck, p. 175.
7. Simcha Paull Raphael, *Jewish Views of the Afterlife* (Jason Aronson, Inc., 1994), p. 137.
8. Fred B. Eiseman, Jr., *Bali Sekala and Niskala,* vol. 2 (Berkeley, Calif.: Periplus Editions, 1990), pp. 115–28.
9. George Gallup, Jr., *Adventures in Immortality* (McGraw Hill, 1982), p. 97.
10. Clark Wissler, *The Social Life of the Blackfoot Indians* (New York: American Museum of Natural History, 1911), p. 144.
11. George Gallup, Jr., *Adventures in Immortality* (McGraw Hill, 1982), p. 199.
12. Denise Lardner Carmody and John Tully Carmody, *Native American Religions* (New York: Paulist Press, 1993), pp. 24–25.
13. Leo Trepp, *The Complete Book of Jewish Observance* (New York: Behrman House/Summit Books, 1980), pp. 332–36.
14. Isaiah 64:3.
15. Masud Kahan, "On Lying Fallow," *Hidden Selves* (I.U. Press, 1983), pp. 183–188.
16. Roberto Assagioli, personal communication.

Chapter 4

1. Mircea Eliade, *The Encyclopedia of Religion,* vol. 5 (Macmillan, 1987), p. 44.
2. Simcha Paull Raphael, p. 107.
3. Andrew Bongiorno, personal communication.
4. Francesca Fremantle and Chogyam Trungpa, *Tibetan Book of the Dead* (Shambala 1992), p. 53.
5. Ibid., p. 60.

6. Ibid., p. 140.

7. Sogyal Rinpoche, *The Tibetan Book of Living and Dying* (Harper Collins, 1992), p. 223.

8. Ma'sumian, pp. 79–80.

9. Ibid., pp. 22–23.

10. Martha G. Anderson, "The Funeral of an Ijo Shrine Priest," *African Arts*, p. 54.

Chapter 5

1. Howard Morphy, *Ancestral Connections* (Chicago: University of Chicago Press, 1991), pp. 221 and 268.

2. Sullivan, *Icanchu's Dream*, p. 528.

3. Revelations 21:9–11.

4. Farnaz Ma'sumian, *Life after Death* (Oneworld, 1995), pp. 32, 38.

5. Ibid., p. 51.

6. Paul Radin, *Primitive Religion* (Dover Publications), pp. 28–29.

7. Ma'sumian, pp. 81 and 83.

8. Ibid., p. 51–53.

9. Edmundo Barbosa, "The Presence of the Gods: Afro-Brazilian Trance Rituals," *Shaman's Drum* (Mid-Summer, 1989), p. 42.

10. Radin, p. 281.

11. John Parker, *The Works of Dionysius the Aeropagite* (Company Publishing, Richwood, 1976), p. 81.

12. Earthspirit for Dolphy, Novato, Calif.; a printed card.

13. Parker, p. 98.

14. Adapted from John Ferguson, ed., *Encyclopedia of Mysticism* (New York: Continuum, 1995), p. 181; Mercea Eliade, ed., *An Encyclopedia of Religion*, vol. 13 (New York: Macmillan, 1987), p. 192–93; and Michael Talbot, *The Holographic Universe* (New York: Harper Collins, 1992), pp. 257–59.

15. Rudolf Steiner, *Life Between Death and Rebirth* (New York: Anthroposophic Press, 1964).

16. Material on Terence McKenna based on personal communication.

17. Ma'sumian, p. 6.

Chapter 6

1. Raymond Araza, "Igbo Concept of Death: Life After Death," Ahiajoku Lecture Colloquium, 1991, pp. 4–5.

2. Lawrence E. Sullivan, *Icanchu's Drum,* p. 309.

3. Sullivan, p. 309.

4. Morphy, p. 255.

5. Lawrence E. Sullivan, ed., *Death after Life and the Soul* (New York: Macmillian, 1989), p. 133.

6. Sri Aurobindo, *The Life Divine,* vol. 19 (Sri Aurobindo Ashram, 1970), pp. 802–03.

7. Dalai Lama, *My Land and My People* (McGraw Hill, 1962), p. 22.

8. Plato, *Laws,* Book X; quoted in Joseph Head and S. L. Cranston, *Reincarnation* (Quest, 1961), pp. 557.

9. Ibid., pp. 557–58.

10. Ibid., p. 556.

11. Ian Stevenson, *Children Who Remember Previous Lives* (University of Virginia Press, 1987), p. 435.

12. Ibid., p. 68.

13. Roger J. Woolger, *Other Lives, Other Selves* (New York: Doubleday, 1987), p. 285.

14. Ibid.

15. Brian Weiss, *Many Masters, Many Lives* (New York: Simon & Schuster, 1988), p. 9.

16. Ibid., p. 10.

17. Ibid., p. 218.

18. Rabbi Yonassam Gershom, *Beyond the Ashes* (ARE Press, 1992), pp. 1–2.

19. Radin, pp. 82–83.

20. Stanislaus Grof, *The Holotropic Mind* (HarperCollins), pp. 121–22.

Chapter 7

1. Karl Menninger, "Hope," *Bulletin of the Menninger Clinic,* 51(5), 1987: 116, 481–91.

2. Carl Jung, *Psychology and Religion: West and East,* vol. 11 (Bollingen Series, Princeton), p. 331.

3. C. R. Snyder, *Children and the Price of Excellence: Hope for the Few or the Many?* (Fifth Annual Ester Katz Rosen Symposium on the Psychological Development of Gifted Children, Lawrence, Kansas: University of Kansas, 1995).

4. E. Stotland, *The Psychology of Hope* (San Francisco: Jossey-Bass, 1960), as defined by Snyder in "Conceptualizing, Measuring, and Nurturing

Hope," *Journal of Counseling and Development,* vol. 73, January–February 1995.

5. Maurice Lamm, *The Power of Hope* (Rawson, 1995), p. 43.

6. Sam Keen, *Hymns to an Unknown God: Awakening the Spirit in Everyday Life* (New York: Bantam, 1994), pp. 257–58.

Bibliography

Abhedananda, Swami. *The Mystery of Death*. Calcutta, India: Ramakrishna Vedanta Math, 1953, 1967, 1978.

Anderson, Martha G. "The Funeral of an Ijo Shrine Priest," *African Arts*.

Anthony, Metropolitan. *Living Prayer*. London: Darton, Longman & Todd Ltd., 1966.

Araza, Dr. Raymond C. *Igbo Concept of Death: Life after Death*. Ahiajoku Lecture Colloquium, 1991.

Ariès, Philippe. *The Hour of Our Death*. New York: Vintage Books, 1981.

————. *Images of Man & Death*. Cambridge, Mass.: Harvard University Press, 1985.

————. *Western Attitudes Toward Death: From the Middle Ages to the Present*. Baltimore, London: The Johns Hopkins University Press, 1974.

Assagioli, Roberto, M.D. *Psychosynthesis*. New York: The Viking Press, 1965.

Aurobindo, Sri. *The Life Divine*, vol. 19. Sri Aurobindo Ashram, 1970.

Bahá'u'lláh and 'Abdu' L-Bahá. *Bahá'í World Faith*. Wilmette, Illinois, USA: Bahá'í Publishing Trust, 1943.

Bahti, Mark. *Navajo Sandpainting Art*. Marceline, Missouri: Walsworth Publishing Company, 1978.

Bailey, Alice A. *Esoteric Healing*, vol. 4, Seven Rays. New York, London: Lucis Publishing Company, 1970.

Barbosa, Edmundo. *Afro-Brazilian Trance Rituals,* Shaman's Drum, #17, 1989.

Beane, Wendell C. and William G. Doty. *Myths, Rites, Symbols*. New York: Harper Touchbooks, 1975.

Beard, Paul. *Hidden Man*. Tasburgh, Norwich, England: Pilgrim Books, 1986.

————. *Living On*. London, Boston, Sydney: George Allen & Unwin, 1980.

————. *Survival of Death*. Tasburgh, Norwich, England: Pilgrims Book Services, 1966.

Berg, Rabbi Philip S. *Reincarnation: Wheels of a Soul*. New York: Research Centre of Kabbalah Press, 1991.

Bernstein, Alan E. *The Formation of Hell*. London: Cornell University Press, 1993.

Besant, Annie and C. W. Leadbeater. *Thought-Forms*. Wheaton, Illinois: The Theosophical Publishing House, 1969.

Biardeau, Madeline. *Hinduism, the Anthropology of a Civilization*. Oxford: Oxford University Press, 1989.

Bloch, Maurice and Jonathan Parry, eds. *Death and the Reincarnation of Life*. Cambridge: Cambridge University Press, 1982.

Brantle, George, ed. *The Religious Experience*, vol. 1–2. Toronto: Ambassador Books, 1964.

Brena, M.D. and F. Steven. *Pain and Religion*. Springfield, Illinois: Charles C. Thomas, 1972.

Budge, E.A. Wallis. *The Book of the Dead*. Arkana: Penguin Books, 1989.

Carmody, Denise Lardner and John Tully Carmody. *Native American Religions*. New York: Paulist Press, 1993.

Cirlot, J.E. *A Dictionary of Symbols*. New York: Philosophical Library, 1962.

Comper, Frances M.N. *The Book of the Craft of Dying*. London: Longmans, Green, 1917.

Coomaraswamy, Ananda K. and Sister Nivedita. *Myths of the Hindus and Buddhists*. New York: Dover Publications, Inc., 1967.

Corbin, H. *Mundus Imaginalis or the Imaginal and the Imagined*. Ipswitch, England, 1972.

Cowan, James G. *The Aborigine Tradition*. Shaftesburg, Dorset, and Rockport, Mass.: Element, 1992.

Crocker, Jon Christopher. *Vital Souls*. Tucson, Arizona: The University of Arizona Press, 1985.

Crookhall, Robert. *Out-of-the-Body Experiences*. Secaucus, New Jersey: The Citadel Press, 1970.

Dalai Lama, The. *My Land and My People*. McGraw Hill, 1962.

Darling, David. *Soul Search: A Scientist Explores the Afterlife*. Villard, 1995.

Davies, Paul. *God and the New Physics*. Simon & Schuster, 1983.

Doore, Gary, Ph.D. *What Survives?* Los Angeles: Jeremy P. Tarcher, 1990.

Dossey, Larry, M.D. *Recovering the Soul*. New York: Bantam Books, 1989.

Driver, Harold E. *Indians of North America*. Chicago: The University of Chicago Press, 1961.

Eadie, Betty J. *Embraced by the Light*. Gold Leaf Press, 1992.

Easwaran, Eknath. *Dialogue With Death*. Nilgiri Press, 1981, 1992.

Edwards, Paul, ed. *The Encyclopedia of Philosophy*, vol. 1, 2, 7, 8. New York: Macmillan, 1967.

Eiseman, Fred B., Jr. *Balie Tekala and Niskala*, vol. 2. Berkeley: Periplus Editions, 1990.

Eisenbud, M.D., Jule. *Paranormal Foreknowledge*. New York: Human Sciences Press, Inc., 1982.

———. *Parapsychology and the Unconscious*. Berkeley: North Atlantic Books, 1983.

———. *PSI and Psychoanalysis*. New York: Grune & Stratton, 1970.

Eliade, Mircea. ed., *The Encyclopedia of Religion*, vol. 13. New York: Macmillan, 1987.

———. *Myths, Dreams, and Mysteries*. Grand Rapids, Philadelphia, St. Louis: Harper Torchbooks, 1957.

———. *The Sacred & the Profane*. New York: HBJ Book, 1957, 1959.

Elkin, A.P. *Aboriginal Men of High Degree*. Rochester, Vermont: Inner Traditions, 1977.

Emmons, George Thornton. *The Tlingit Indians*. Seattle: University of Washington Press, 1991.

Enright, D.J. *The Oxford Book of Death*. New York: Oxford University Press, 1983.

Epstein, M.D., Mark. *Thoughts Without a Thinker*. New York: Basic Books, 1995.

Evans-Wentz, W. Y. *The Tibetan Book of the Dead*. Oxford University Press, 1960.

Farthing, Geoffrey. *When We Die*. India, USA: Theosophical Publishing House London Ltd., 1968.

Ferguson, John. *Encyclopedia of Mysticism and the Mystery Religions*. New York: The Seabury Press, 1975.

Ferrucci, Piero. *What We May Be*. New York: Putnam, 1982.

Frankl, Viktor E. *Man's Search for Meaning*. Washington Square Press, 1984.

Frazer, Sir James George. *The Golden Bough*. New York: Macmillan, 1922.

Freeman, Eileen Elias. *Touched by Angels*. New York: Warner Books, 1993.

Fremantle, Francesca and Chogyam Trungpa, trans. with commentary. *The Tibetan Book of the Dead*. Boston: Shambhala, 1992.

Gallup, George, Jr. *Adventures in Immortality*. McGraw-Hill, 1982.

Gaskell, G.A. *Dictionary of All Scriptures and Myths*. New York: The Julian Press, Inc., 1960.

Gershom, Rabbi Yonassan. *Beyond the Ashes*. Virginia: A.R.E. Press, 1992.

Glaze, Anita, J. *Art & Death in a Senufo Village*. Bloomington, Indiana University Press, 1981.

Goldstein, Joseph. *The Experience of Insight*. Boston: Shambhala, 1983.

Gotshalk, Richard. *Bhagavad Gita*. Delhi: Motilal Banarsidass, 1985.

Govinda, Lama Anagarika. *Foundations of Tibetan Mysticism*. New York: Samuel Weiser, 1969.

Grof, Stanislaus, M.D. and Joan Halifax, Ph.D. *The Holotropic Mind*. HarperCollins, 1993.

————. *The Human Encounter With Death*. New York: E.P. Dutton, 1963.

Grollman, Earl A. *Concerning Death, A Practical Guide for the Living*. Boston: Beacon Press, 1974.

Haleui, Zev ben Shimon. *Kabbalah and Psychology*. New York: Samuel Weiser, 1986.

Hall, Manly Palmer. *Reincarnation, The Cycle of Necessity*. Los Angeles: The Philosophical Research Society, 1946.

————. *The Way of Heaven*. Los Angeles: The Philosophical Research Society, 1946, 1974, 1990.

Harner, Michael. *The Way of the Shaman*. New York: Bantam Books, 1980.

Hastings, Arthur. *With the Tongues of Men and Angels*. Holt, Rinehart, and Winston, 1991.

Head, Joseph and S.L. Cranston, eds. and comps. *Reincarnation An East-West Anthology*. Wheaton, Ill.: The Theosophical Publishing House, 1961.

Herzog, Edgar. *Psyche and Death*. Dallas, Texas: Spring Publications, 1983.

Hick, John H. *Death & Eternal Life*. New York: Harper & Row, 1976.

Holbein, Hans. *The Dance of Death*. New York: Dover Publications, 1971.

Holmes, Dr. Jesse Herman and The Holmes Research Team. *As We See It from Here*. North Carolina: Meta Science Corp. Publications, 1980.

Holzer, Hans. *The Reincarnation*. New York: Harper & Row, 1974.

Hope, Murray. *The Psychology of Ritual*. Dorset: Element Books, 1988.

Huxley, Aldous. *The Doors of Perception*. New York: Colophon Books, 1954.

Huxley, Laura Archera. *This Timeless Moment*. Millbrae, CA: Celestial Arts, 1968.

Inglis, Brian. *The Unknown Guest*. Great Britain: Coronet Books, 1989.

Isaiah 64:3.

Iverson, Jeffrey. *In Search of the Dead*. San Francisco: Harper, 1992.

Jacobi, Jolande. *Complex, Archetype, Symbol*. New Jersey: Princeton University Press, 1959.

Jaffé, Aniela. *Apparitions*. Irving, Texas: Spring Publications, 1979.

Jahn, Robert G. and Brenda J. Dunne. *Margins of Reality*. New York: Harcourt Brace Jovanovich, 1987.

James, William. *The Varieties of Religious Experience*. Penguin Books, 1982.

———. *The Will to Believe*. New York: Dover Publications, Inc., 1956.

Jobes, Gertrude. *Dictionary of Mythology, Folklore and Symbols*, vol. 1, 2. The Scarecrow Press, 1962.

Jung, Carl G. *Memories, Dreams, and Reflections*. Vintage Books, 1963.

———. *Psychology and Religion: West and East*, vol. 11. Bollingen Series, Princeton, N.J.

Kahan, Masud. "On Lying Fallow," *Hidden Selves*. I.U. Press, 1983.

Kaku, Michio. *Hyperspace*. New York: Anchor Doubleday, 1994.

Kapleau, Philip. *The Wheel of Life & Death*. New York: Anchor Books, Doubleday, 1989.

Karagulla, M.D., Shaficia. *Breakthrough to Creativity*. Santa Monica, CA: DeVorss, 1967.

Kardec, Alan. *The Gospel According to Spiritism*. London: The Headquarters Publishing Company, Ltd., 1987.

———. *The Spirits Book*. trans. Anna Blackwell. Boston: Colby and Rich, Publishers, 1875.

KatÑ, BunnÑ, YoshirÑ Tamura, KÑjirÑ Miyasaka, trans. Revisions by W. E. Soothill, Wilhelm Schiffer, Pier P. Del Campana. *The Threefold Lotus Sutra*. New York: John Weatherhill, Inc., 1975.

Katz, Richard. *Boiling Energy*. Cambridge, Mass.: Harvard University Press, 1982.

———. *The Straight Path*. New York: A Merloyd Lawrence Book, 1993.

Keen, Sam. *Hymns to an Unknown God: Awakening the Spirit in Everyday Life*. New York: Bantam, 1994.

Keesing, Roger M. *Kwaio Religion*. New York: Columbia University Press: 1982.

Kelsey, Morton T. *Afterlife: The Other Side of Dying*. New York: Crossroad, 1979.

Khan, Inayat. *Sufi Teachings*. England, Servire Publishers, 1963.

Koestler, Arthur. *The Act of Creation*. New York: Macmillan, 1964.

Kramer, Kenneth. *The Sacred Art of Dying*. New York: Paulist Press, 1988.

Kübler-Ross, Elisabeth. *Death Is of Vital Importance*. Barrytown, New York: Station Hill Press, 1995.

———. *Death: The Final Stage of Growth*. New Jersey: Prentice-Hall, Inc., 1975.

———. *On Children and Death*. New York: Collier Books, 1983.

———. *On Death and Dying*. New York: Macmillan, 1969.

———. *On Life after Death*. Berkeley, CA: Celestial Arts, 1991.

———. *Questions and Answers on Death and Dying*. New York: Collier Books, 1974.

Kung, Hans. *Eternal Life: Life After Death as a Medical, Philosophical, and Theological Problem*. New York: Doubleday, 1984.

Lamm, Maurice. *The Power of Hope*. Rawson, 1995.

Lauf, Detlef Ingo. *Secret Doctrines of the Tibetan Books of the Dead*. Boston: Shambhala, 1989.

Leadbeater, C. W. *The Inner Life,* vol. 2. Wheaton, Illinois: The Theosophical Publishing House, 1967.

———. *The Masters and the Path*. Wheaton, Illinois: The Theosophical Publishing House, 1975.

Leeuw, J. J. Van Der. *The Conquest of Illusion*. Wheaton, Ill.: The Theosophical Publishing House, 1966.

Loudon, John and James C. Parabola Odell. *Myth: The Quest for Meaning,* vol. 2, Issue 1. New York: The Tamarack Press, 1977.

MacGregor, Geddes. *Images of Afterlife*. New York: Paragon House, 1992.

———. *Reincarnation in Christianity*. Wheaton, Ill.: The Theosophical Publishing House, 1978.

Mannheim, Ralph and R.F.C. Hull, trans. *Spiritual Disciplines*. New York: Pantheon Books, 1960.

Martin, Joel and Patricia Romanowski. *We Don't Die*. New York: Putnam, 1988.

Mason, J. Alden. *The Ancient Civilizations of Peru*. Penguin Books, 1957, 1968.

Ma'sumian, Farnaz. *Life After Death: A Study of the Afterlife in World Religions*. Oxford: Oneworld, 1995.

McIntyre, Loren. *The Incredible Incas and Their Timeless Land*. Washington, D.C.: National Geographic Society, 1975.

McKenna, Terence. *Food of the Gods*. New York: Bantam Books, 1992.

——. *True Hallucinations*. San Francisco: Harper, 1993.

Menninger, Karl. "Hope," *Bulletin of the Menninger Clinic*. 51(5), 1987: 116, 481–91.

Miller, Stuart. *Hot Springs*. Viking, 1971.

Mitchell, Stephen. *A Book of Psalms*. New York: HarperCollins, 1993.

Monroe, Robert A. *Ultimate Journey*. New York: Doubleday, 1994.

Moody, Raymond, M.D. and Paul Perry. *Life After Life*. Toronto, New York: Bantam Books, 1977.

——. *The Light Beyond*. New York: Bantam Books, 1988.

——. *Reunions*. New York: Villard Books, 1993.

Morphy, Howard. *Ancestral Connections*. Chicago: The University of Chicago Press, 1991.

Morse, Melvin, M.D. and Paul Perry. *Closer to the Light*. New York: Ivy Books, 1990.

Mullin, Glenn H. *Selected Works of the Dalai Lama II*. Ithaca, New York: Snow Lion Publications, 1982, 1985.

Murphet, Howard. *Beyond Death: The Undiscovered Country*. Wheaton, Illinois: The Theosophical Publishing House, 1990.

Murphy, Michael. *The Future of the Body*. Los Angeles: Jeremy P. Tarcher, 1992.

Murray, Jocelyn. *Cultural Atlas of Africa*. New York: An Equinox Book, 1989.

Murti, T.R.V. *The Central Philosophy of Buddhism*. London: George Allen & Unwin Ltd., 1960.

Needleman, Jacob. *A Sense of the Cosmos*. New York: Doubleday & Company, Inc., 1975.

Neiman, Carol and Emily Goldman. *Afterlife*. England: Viking Studio Books, 1994.

Noel, Daniel C. "Soul and Earth: Traveling with Jung Toward an Archetypal Ecology," *Quadrant: The Journal of Contemporary Jungian Thought*, vol. 23. 2:67.

Nuland, Sherwin B. *How We Die*. New York: Knopf, 1994.

O'Flaherty, Wendy Doniger. *Hindu Myths*. New York: Penguin Books, 1978.

O'Grady, Joan. *The Prince of Darkness*. Longmead, Shaftesbury, Dorset: Element Books, 1989.

Otto, Rudolf. *The Idea of the Holy*. Oxford University Press, 1958.

Parfitt, Will. *The Qaba Lah*. Shaftesbury, Dorset and Rockport, Mass.: Element, 1991.

Parker, John, ed. *The Works of Dionysius the Areopagite*. Merrick, N.Y.: Richmond, 1976.

Pauchard, Albert. *The Other World*. London: Van Duren Press Ltd., 1973.

Pereira, José. *Hindu Theology: A Reader*. Garden City, New York: Image Books, 1976.

Phillips, David R., Todd E. Rath, and Lisa M. Wagner. "Psychology and Survival," *The Lancet*. 342 (November 6, 1993).

Plato. *Laws*. Book X.

Po, Li, trans. by Sam Hamill, from Stephen Mitchell, ed. *The Enlightened Heart: An Anthology of Sacred Poetry*. New York: Harper Perennial, 1989.

Poloma, Margaret M. and George H. Gallup, Jr. *Varieties of Prayer*. Philadelphia: Trinity Press International, 1991.

Purucker, G. de. *The Esoteric Tradition,* vol. 1, 2. Pasadena, CA: Theosophical University Press, 1935.

Rabten, Geshe. *The Preliminary Practices of Tibetan Buddhism*. Dharamsala, H.P.: Library of Tibetan Works and Archives, 1974.

Radhakrishnan, Sarvedalli and Charles A. Moore. *Indian Philosophy*. Princeton, New Jersey: Princeton University Press, 1957.

Radin, Paul. *Primitive Religion*. New York: Dover Publications, Inc., 1957.

Ramacharaka, Yogi. *The Life Beyond Death*. Chicago, Illinois: Yogi Publication Society, 1937.

Raphael, Simcha Paull. *Jewish Views of the Afterlife*. Northvale, New Jersey: Jason Aronson, Inc., 1994.

Raudive, Konstantin, Ph.D. *Breakthrough*. Garrards Cross: Colin Smythe, 1971.

Reat, N. Ross. *Origins of Indian Psychology*. Berkeley, CA: Asian Humanities Press, 1990.

Redhouse, James, W. *Legends of the Sufis*. London: The Theosophical Publishing House, Ltd., 1976.

Reimer, Jack, ed. *Jewish Reflections on Death*. New York: Schocken Books, 1974.

Revelations 21:9–11.

Ring, Kenneth. *Heading Toward Omega*. New York: William Morrow, Inc., 1985.

———. *Life at Death*. New York: William Morrow, Inc., 1980.

————. *The Omega Project.* New York: William Morrow, Inc., 1995.

————. Gary Dove, ed. *What Survives.* Los Angeles: Tarcher, 1990.

Rogo, D. Scott. *Leaving the Body.* New York: Prentice-Hall, 1983.

————. *NAD: A Study of Some Unusual "Other-World" Experiences.* New York University Books, 1970.

Rose, Fr. Seraphim. *The Soul after Death.* Platina, CA: Saint Herman of Alaska Brotherhood, 1993.

Ross, Nancy Wilson. *Buddhism, A Way of Life and Thought.* New York: Vintage Books, 1980.

Sabiers, Karl, M.A. *Where Are the Dead?* Los Angeles: Christian Pocket Books, 1959.

Sassoon, George and Rodney Dale. *The Kabbalah Decoded.* London: Duckworth, 1978.

Scholem, Gershom, G. *On the Kabbalah and Its Symbolism.* New York: Schocken Books, 1960.

Sheldrake, Rupert. *The Presence of the Past.* New York: Vintage Books, 1988.

————. *The Rebirth of Nature, the Greening of Science and God.* New York: Bantam Books, 1991.

Snyder, C. R., Susie Simpson, Florence Ybasco, Tyrone F. Borders, Michael A. Babyak, and Raymond Higgins. *Children and the Price of Excellence: Hope for the Few or the Many?* Fifth Annual Ester Katz Rosen Symposium on the Psychological Development of Gifted Children. Lawrence, Kansas: University of Kansas, 1995.

————. "Development and Validation of the Hope Scale," *Journey of Personality and Social Psychology.* In press.

Sogyal, Rinpoche. *The Tibetan Book of Living and Dying.* San Francisco: Harper, 1992.

Sonsino, Rifat and Daniel B. Syme. *What Happens after I Die.* New York: UAHC Press, 1990.

Speck, Frank Gouldsmith. *A Study of the Delaware Indian Big House Ceremony.* Harrisburg, Penn.: Historical Commission, 1931.

Steiner, Rudolf. *Life Between Death & Rebirth.* New York: Anthroposophic Press, 1968.

Steinsaltz, Adin. *The Thirteen Petalled Rose.* New York: Basic Books, Inc., Publishers, 1980.

Stevenson, Ian, M.D. *Cases of Reincarnation,* vol. 1–4. The University Press of Virginia, 1975, 1977, 1980, 1983.

————. *Children Who Remember Previous Lives.* The University Press of Virginia, 1987.

Stotland, E. *The Psychology of Hope.* San Francisco: Jossey-Bass, 1960.

Stuart, Gene S. *The Mighty Aztecs.* Washington, D.C.: National Geographic Society, 1981.

Stuart, George E. and Gene S. Stuart. *The Mysterious Maya.* Washington, D.C.: National Geographic Society, 1977.

Sullivan, Lawrence E. ed., *Death, Afterlife, and the Soul.* New York: Macmillan, 1989.

————. *Icanchu's Drum.* New York: Macmillan, 1988.

Talbot, Michael. *The Holographic Universe.* New York: Harper Collins, 1992.

Thompson, Keith. *Angels and Aliens.* New York: Fawcett Columbine, 1991.

Thompson, Robert Farris. *Face of the Gods.* Prestel, Munich: The Museum for African Art, New York, 1993.

————. *Flash of the Spirit.* New York: Vintage Books, 1983.

Throckmorton, Spencer. *Transformations: Stone Figures from Mezcala/ Chontal.* Sante Fe: Kubaba Books, 1991.

Thurman, Robert. *The Holy Teaching of Uimalakàrti.* The Pennsylvania State University Press, 1976.

————. *Wisdom and Compassion: The Sacred Art of Tibet,* New York: Harry N. Abrams, 1991.

Tipler, Frank J. *The Physics of Immortality.* New York: Doubleday, 1994.

Trachtenberg, Joshua. *Jewish Magic and Superstition.* New York: A Temple Book, 1987.

Turner, Alice K. *The History of Hell.* New York: Harcourt Brace & Company, 1993.

Versluis, Arthur. *Native American Traditions.* Queensland: Element, 1993.

Volkman, Toby Alice. *Feasts of Honor.* Urbana and Chicago: University of Illinois Press, 1985.

Von-Franz, Marie-Louise. *On Dreams and Death.* Berkeley, CA: Shambhala, 1984.

Waldrop, M. Mitchell. *Complexity.* New York: Simon & Schuster, 1992.

Walters, John. *The Essence of Buddhism.* New York: Thomas Y. Crowell Company, 1964.

Weiss, Brian L. *Many Lives, Many Masters.* New York: Simon & Schuster, 1988.

Wilber, Ken. *The Spectrum of Consciousness.* Wheaton, Ill: The Theosophical Publishing House, 1977.

Wilson, Ian. *The Afterdeath Experience*. New York: William Morrow, 1987.

Winnipeg Art Gallery. *The Eskimo Shamanism and Art*. Jean Blodgett, Curator of Eskimo Art, 1978.

Wissler, Clark. *The Social Life of the Blackfoot Indians*. New York: American Museum of Natural History, 1911.

Wolf, Fred Alan, Ph.D. *The Dreaming Universe*. New York: Simon & Schuster, 1994.

———. *Parallel Universes*. New York: Simon & Schuster, Inc., 1988.

Woolger, Roger J. *Other Lives, Other Selves*. New York: Doubleday, 1987.

Zaleski, Carol. *Otherworld Journeys*. Oxford University Press, 1987.

Zimmer, Heinrich. *Philosophies of India*. New Jersey: Princeton University Press, 1951.

Index

components of, 163–64
physical suffering and, 164
houris, 126
hun, 67
hypnosis, 152, 155

Ifa, 192
Igbo:
reincarnation of, 58, 139–40
senior researcher of, 193
Ijo:
guides of, 128–29
mortuary rituals of, 104
senior researcher of, 194
illusion, reality as, 66, 101–2, 144
imaginal realm, 46–48, 65
incorporation, 39
India, 18, 69–70, 94–95, 114–17,
151, 190
Nath in, 199–200
senior researchers in, 198–200
Sikh in, 198, 199
vital imagination in, 54, 55, 58
see also Hinduism
Indonesia, 18, 35–37, 102, 122, 190
senior researchers in, 200
see also Sulawesi
Institute for the Study of the
Afterdeath, 18–19, 21, 189–202
databases of, 201–2
senior researchers of, 189–200
Institute of Noetic Sciences, 201–2
Instrumented Communication, 77–78
intentions, 96–97, 98
interests, unusual, 151
Inuit Eskimo, 121–22
Inventory, Afterdeath, 169–88
Iran, 103
Iroko, Amelie Degbelo, 190–91, 193
Islam, 147
group resurrection in, 149
heaven of, 63, 82, 103
hell of, 82, 103

judgment stage in, 103, 149
see also Sufism
Iware, A. U., 192

James, dying process of, 25, 29–30,
31, 37, 157–58, 162, 163, 165
Japan, 54–55
Jesus Christ, 123, 126, 129, 149
Joanne, dying process of, 25, 32–34,
79
John of Patmos, 123, 126
Jonathan, waiting place and, 81–82
Josie, reincarnation and, 135–39,
150, 158–60
Judaism, 67, 147
group resurrection in, 149
heaven of, 124–25, 126
Holocaust victims and, 155–57
judgment stage in, 91–92
mortuary rituals of, 70–71, 72, 79
reincarnation in, 149, 159
stage of possibilities in, 124–25
judgment stage, 19, 20, 85–112, 120,
126
absence of, 89, 90, 108–11
of ancient Egyptians, 90, 91
angels in, 91–92
in art, 89, 92
bridges in, 89, 102–4
in Buddhism, 89, 93–94, 98–102
Challenge Method of, 98–102, 128
in Christianity, 90, 92–93
context of, 104–5
Doreen and, 86–87, 88, 104
Eleanor and, 108–11
Esalen Institute and, 106–8
Evolutionary Method of, 96–98
in goal-oriented systems, 89
in Hinduism, 92, 93–95
in Islam, 103, 149
in Judaism, 91–92
judges in, 87, 89, 90, 96, 99, 103,
104

About the Author

Sukie Miller, Ph.D., a psychotherapist, is one of the first researchers to study the cross-cultural dimensions of the afterdeath. Dr. Miller, an early director of Esalen Institute, has been a member of the Jung Institute of San Francisco and the Board of Medical Quality Assurance for the State of California. In 1972 she founded and directed the pioneering Institute for the Study of Humanistic Medicine. She is currently founder and director of the Institute for the Study of the Afterdeath.